THE THEME OF THE
PARTITION

DR. EKTA DIXIT

BLUEROSE PUBLISHERS
India | U.K.

Copyright © Dr Ekta Dixit 2024

All rights reserved by author. No part of this publication may be reproduced, stored in a retrieval system or transmitted in any form or by any means, electronic, mechanical, photocopying, recording or otherwise, without the prior permission of the author. Although every precaution has been taken to verify the accuracy of the information contained herein, the publisher assume no responsibility for any errors or omissions. No liability is assumed for damages that may result from the use of information contained within.

BlueRose Publishers takes no responsibility for any damages, losses, or liabilities that may arise from the use or misuse of the information, products, or services provided in this publication.

For permissions requests or inquiries regarding this publication, please contact:

BLUEROSE PUBLISHERS
www.BlueRoseONE.com
info@bluerosepublishers.com
+91 8882 898 898
+4407342408967

ISBN: 978-93-5819-385-5

Cover design: Tahira
Typesetting: Tanya Raj Upadhyay

First Edition: February 2024

Partition of our beloved motherland and the resulting aftermath will always corrode the painful memories of the past. I cannot begin to explain how objectively and respectfully the author has viewed the existing classic literature upon the theme of partition. Every book that the author has picked and described has a heart of its own. It's almost like the work of the author is spotless, nearly perfect. Partition was not just about dividing boundaries but it was also about dividing the historical bond that existed between the two prominent communities settled in those lands. It caused mayhem, tremendous havoc, extreme hatred, brutality and communal wars, the sensations of which are still very much present and have become the very fabric of the strained relationship the Hindu and the Muslim community share with one another, even in the present times. However, times of distress also unite the ones who believe in uplifting humanity, regardless of their religion. Even in the toughest times during the partition, there were those who chose humanity above other things. The master class pieces of literature work that the author has shed light upon in her paper are just too good. This manuscript, although objective, was also very moving. The way the author has given a detailed description of the themes and events and the characters of the books are soul touching. It was a delight reading it.

Congratulations to the author!

ACKNOWLEDGEMENTS

It is a privilege for me to be able to extend my gratitude to all those who assisted me in the preparation of this book. My gratitude goes in the first place to my supervisor, Dr. Supriya Shukla. My supervisor's guidance and consistent support always encouraged me to do better. She always gave me valuable advice and took a keen interest in my work to improve its quality. It is my pleasant duty to express my warm regards to my father Shri. Prabha Kant Tiwari and my mother Smt. Vinod Kumari for their blessings which made me confident of completing my work successfully. I want to express my gratefulness to my father-in-law Late Shri. Virendra Kumar Dixit and my husband Mr. Subodh Dixit who always gave me moral support and never let me deviate my attention from the work. I extend my gratitude to my teacher Miss Shailja Kumar who rendered her assistance by constantly encouraging me during the work and always motivating me to make sincere efforts to complete the work. Last, but not least, there are many I owe a great deal for the valuable help they rendered to me in the development of this work in various ways.

Dated:
Dr. Ekta Dixit

PREFACE

The cataclysmic episode of the partition which changed the entire course of history of the Indian sub-continent was often vividly brought to life by the partition stories that I heard from my grandfather. The horrific tales narrated by him filled me with a deep desire to delve deep into this period. Subsequent meetings in my growing years with those who had been affected by the partition directly or indirectly further fuelled my desire and set me on an earnest quest to find out more.

History, being creative fiction, casts a spell over many an Indian English novelist. Writers affected by the freedom movement and the partition, generally throw light upon the freedom struggle and the gruesome event of the partition with a critical perspective revealing the macabre aspects of the struggle. Imbued with the spirit of nationalism most of these writers who witnessed the gruesome event were evidently in mental turmoil which finds expression through their novels of that period. There are many renowned writers who have chosen partition as a theme for their writing. Attia Hosain, Manohar Malgaonkar, Chaman Nahal, and Bapsi Sidhwa are some such writers who have taken partition as a backdrop for their novels.

The present study also intends to investigate the portrayal of different aspects of the Partition. It aims to explore how the novelists make use of their past experiences and compel the readers to draw their own conclusions. Through their works, the writers of the partition fiction highlight the difficulties, disturbances, and distress faced by people during the partition. The feeling of being uprooted is also poignantly brought out in all the novels. However, they also leave a ray of hope for the reunion of both the communities in future. What is striking and common among all the partition novelists taken up for study is that they have all focused on human values. Human relationships have depicted that even in the midst of all the animalism and beastliness that prevailed moral and humanitarian values also remained. Every novelist emphasises the humanitarian angle which is presented through special characters. The main aim of this book is to understand the politics and circumstances during the partition in the novels of Attia Hosain, Manohar Malgaonkar, Chaman Nahal, and Bapsi Sidhwa from a fresh perspective.

TABLE OF CONTENTS

Introduction 1

Historical Perspective on The Theme of The Partition 28

Sunlight On A Broken Column 47

A Bend In The Ganges 83

Azadi 109

Ice-Candy-Man 157

Conclusion 187

Bibliography 198

Summary 207

INTRODUCTION

History is the depository of great actions, the witness of what is past, the example and instructor of the present, and the monitor of the future.

----- Cervantes

In the light of the observation by Cervantes, one can trace the events that led to the partition, the ensuing miseries, and the tremendous upheavals which tore the country. The events that led to the partition and served as a 'monitor to the future' cannot be understood without turning the pages of the past. Life is seen in the framework of history in a historical novel. History has provided a context for fiction. The historical novel is a creative portrayal of history. It is the past state of affairs that affect the human experience. The purpose of a historian is to filter down the facts and figures from the past, but the objective of a historical writer is to generate the characters who recreate history in the present. They are as much influenced by history as they themselves exert an influence on it. Fiction has a very natural tendency of presenting the lives of the poor delineate rigid class structures and imperial feudalism. The fusion of history and fiction results in a human story rather than a pool of facts and figures. The use of history depends upon the novelist. A good novelist uses historical material only to the extent it is essential to his fiction. He takes from history general ideas and outlines and assimilates them into his plot in such a way that they become a part of his fictional world. In the historical novel history becomes an eternal presence in fiction. The aim of the historical novel is to depict the predominant and crucial events of history.

The partition of the subcontinent has influenced India's past and present. The origin of Pakistan can be traced to the pre-British period but its complete propagation took place on the eve of the British departure from India. The partition holocaust in 1947 was the pinnacle and consummation of the British intrigues, the culmination of a separatist process initiated by a colonial government to foster and promote its imperial interests. However, the other prevailing opinion is that Pakistan came into being because Muslims constituted a separate nation and their animosity with the Hindus started long before the British surfaced on the scene. Many interpretations have been put forward concerning the causes that have paved the way for Muslim separatism culminating in the partition.

British rule became established in eastern India around the mid-eighteenth century, and by the early part of the nineteenth century, the British had tightened their grip over considerable portions of the country. Hindu -Muslim unity was visible in the revolt of 1857 against the British. But the British crushed the revolt. They realised that the real strength of the revolt was the Hindu-Muslim unity and it was substantiated when cow slaughter had been proscribed at some places wherever the revolt was successful. So, the

British government adopted a rancorous and malevolent attitude towards the Muslims by hanging 27,000 Muslims alone. The seed of separatism had been sown when the spiteful British adopted a malicious attitude towards the Muslims to teach them a lesson so that they would not dare to oppose the British. For fulfilling their purpose the British provided many facilities to the Hindus like government jobs and opportunities in education. To embitter the minds of the Muslims, the British interchanged Persian script with Devnagri and Urdu language with Hindi. The Hindus took advantage of this and set a new milestone. After many years in 1875, the British felt the imbalance, and to encourage the sense of separatism, they patronized the Muhammadan Anglo-Oriental College of Sayyid Ahmed Khan. At first, Sayyid Ahmed Khan had healthy communal relations with the Hindus but for the advancement of his community, he changed his perspectives and regarded the British as the defender of the Muslims. The British did nothing to dismiss this view. Instead, they were exhilarated by the disunity between both communities. To encourage the trend of separatism between the two communities, the British decided to support the Muslims in full swing. In this process the fanatic Hindus were eager to intensify the hatred through the Hindu revival movement and 'Shuddhi sangathan' in which they intended to convert non-Hindus into Hindus.

The Indian political system revived after the formation of the Indian League in 1857 and of the Indian Association in 1876. These two organisations differed from each other on the basis of principles. The aim of the Indian League was to compel the Indians to participate in the administration of the country along with the British with all loyalty to the British crown. Indian Association convened an All India Conference at Calcutta. From this emerged the idea of the establishment of the Indian National Congress. With the cooperation of the retired British officer Sir Allen Hume, Indian leaders like Dadabhai Nowroji, Badruddin Tayyabji, Pheroze Shah Mehta, and others established the Indian National Congress in 1885. The first session of the Congress was held in Bombay on 28 December 1885. In the later 19th century, the only aim of all the organizations was to get employment for Indians to high posts in public services, the establishment of representative institutions, and government. It was the Indian National Congress that had given the thought and view of self-government within the empire. But it was also a fact that the leaders of the Congress like Dadabhai Naoroji, Pheroze Shah Mehta, Madan Mohan Malviya, and Gopal Krishna Gokhale were the product of the English education and they had genuine respect for the British culture.

At the end of the 19th century, the Congress felt a 'divine dispensation' about the British government but in spite of their faith and altruism, the British had exploited the country, and India was getting poorer and poorer every day. Later moderate leaders like Dadabhai Naoroji and Gopal Krishna Gokhale blamed the British government for the economic ruin of India. Instead of the faith of the old leaders in Western culture and philosophy and in the British sense of justice, the new leaders like Bal Gangadhar Tilak, Lala Lajpat Rai, Bipin Chandra Pal, Aurobindo Ghosh asserted their faith in the culture, tradition, and philosophy of their own country. Tilak persuaded Indians to raise their voice in favour of self-reliance and self-help and disassociate themselves from the government. This call for action and non-cooperation became the motto of the new phase of the Indian freedom struggle. These Extremists had transformed the sense of freedom. Freedom for them meant self-government or *Purna Swaraj* and the end of all relations with the British. The Extremists did not support violence but the terrorist movement which also fought for freedom differed from the Congress in their method. The terrorist movement trained the terrorists for armed action, terrorised government officials, and went on to the extent of killing them. Gandhi differed from others in his way of getting freedom as he wanted to emphasise more on the moral elevation of the people of India for attaining complete freedom. This was opposed by leaders such as Tilak and Lala Lajpat Rai, who sought quick action towards freedom.

Muslims were not wholeheartedly taking part in the freedom struggle because they constituted a quarter of a third of the population, outnumbered by the Hindus. Early meetings of the Congress contained a minority of Muslims, mostly belonging to rich, powerful, and educated Muslim families. In 1906, a delegation of Muslim leaders headed by the Aga Khan called on the new Viceroy of India, Lord Minto, to assure him of their loyalty and to ask for assurances that in any political reforms, they would be protected from the Hindus. So, many of the same leaders met in Dhaka on 30th December 1906 and founded the All-India Muslim League under the leadership of Aga Khan, president of the Muslim League. Along with him, the other founders were Khwaja Salimullah, Syed Ahmad Khan, and Vikar-ul-Mulk. The All-India Muslim League was the first platform which prophesied that their interests were different from the Hindus. Its political activities were not against the British but against the Hindus. In its earliest years, however, the League was not influential. Even Jinnah opposed it and wrote a letter to the editor of the newspaper *Gujarati*, "asking what right the members of the delegation had to speak for Indian Muslims, as they were unelected and self-appointed". Aga Khan later wrote that it was "freakishly ironic" that Jinnah, who would lead the League to independence, "came out in bitter hostility toward all that I and my friends had done ... He said that our principle of separate electorates was dividing the nation against itself."(Wikipedia)Lord Minto refused to consider it as the Muslim community's representative but later they used it to "divide the nationalist ranks and check the growing unity among Indians by encouraging the growth of communalism" (*Partition Perspectives*, Rao, 9) behind the Minto-Morley Reforms in 1909. In order to suppress and humiliate the Hindus, the British encouraged the Muslims to go against the Hindus. The British government's creation of a separate Muslim electorate was a big threat to the Hindu leaders. In order to protect the rights of the Hindus, the Punjab Hindu Sabha was established in 1909 by Lala Lajpat Rai, Lal Chand, and Shadi Lal. It was a forerunner for the formation of the All India Hindu Sabha which was founded in 1914 in Amritsar and established its headquarters in Haridwar. The early leaders of the Hindu Mahasabha were prominent nationalists and educationalists like Pandit Madan Mohan Malaviya, who founded the Benaras Hindu University, and Lala Lajpat Rai. The prime objectives of the Mahasabha were the education and economic development of the Hindus as well as the reconversion of the Muslims to Hinduism.

Mohammad Ali Jinnah, later a leading political figure and founder of Pakistan, commenced his political career by attending the Congress's twentieth annual meeting, in Bombay in December 1904. He was a member of the moderate group in the Congress. He generated his image as the ambassador of Hindu Muslim unity. He followed leaders like Mehta, Naoroji, and Gopal Krishna Gokhale in attaining self-government.Gokhale, a Hindu, later stated that Jinnah "has true stuff in him, and that freedom from all sectarian prejudice which will make him the best ambassador of Hindu–Muslim Unity."(Wikipedia)

In December 1912, Jinnah addressed the annual meeting of the Muslim League but not as a member. The fidelity of Jinnah was challenged in the Congress after the death of Mehta and Gokhale in 1915. Yet, Jinnah worked to bring the Congress and League together. In 1916, Jinnah joined the Muslim League and became the president. The two organisations, Congress and the Muslim League signed the Lucknow Pact. It was the only occasion in modern Indian history in which the Muslim League and the Congress came to a voluntary agreement about the political future of India. The Pact granted the Muslims many of the safeguards which they had demanded, including separate electorates and 'weightage' in the Legislative Councils of those provinces in which they formed a minority of the population. However, despite the hopes which it raised, the Lucknow Pact had only a temporary effect on the Muslim-Hindu relations. (history today.com) Another important part of the freedom struggle was the foundation of the Home Rule Leagues by Tilak and Annie Besant, an Irish scholar, in 1916 in which Jinnah played an important role. The objectives of these two Leagues, which acted independently but which were not opposed to each other, were to persuade the British to grant full self- government to the Indians.

After the foundation of the Hindu Mahasabha, the gap between the two communities had widened. The event that brought them close was Khilafat Movement. It was launched by Muslims in 1919 against the British and to protect the Ottoman Empire after the First World War. When the Khalifa of the Islamic world lost his temporal authority, the traditional Muslims grew outraged with the British who were responsible for the condition and whom the Muslims in India were supporting in a docile manner. It won the support of the predominant Hindu Congress movement because of its anti-British overtones. Mahatma Gandhi took the opportunity to unite the two large communities by supporting the Khilafat movement and launching the Non-cooperation movement. Gandhi called upon the Muslims to adopt the Congress method of non-violence and non-cooperation in their fight against the British. The best result of the movement was the dwindling of communal tension. Being largely a Muslim religious movement, the Khilafat movement received good response and became a part of the wider Indian independence movement. Gandhi was introduced by Ali brothers and Azad to the Muslims. But Jinnah condemned Gandhi's Khilafat advocacy as he saw it as an endorsement of religious zealotry. The non-cooperation movement aimed to challenge the colonial, economic and power structure, which would force the British authorities to take notice of the demands of the independence movement. Members of both communities had responded in a positive way and went hand in hand. But Jinnah regarded Gandhi's proposed *satyagraha* campaign as political anarchy, and believed that self-government should be secured through constitutional means. He opposed Gandhi, but the tide of Indian opinion was against him. Jinnah did not attend the subsequent League meeting, held in the same city, which passed a similar resolution. The Khilafat movement distorted by late 1922 when Turkey gained a more favourable diplomatic position and moved toward secularism. By 1924 Turkey simply abolished the roles of Sultan and Caliph. After the failure of Khilafat Movement, the Congress decided that Non Cooperation was the only way out for India. The other reasons to start the Non-cooperation movement were that Gandhi had lost faith in constitutional methods and turned from co-operator of British Rule to Non-Co-operator. It was the hit back at the British who instigated and were responsible for the Jallianwala Bagh massacre and other violence in Punjab. The breakdown of the non-co-operation movement brought to an end the Hindu Muslim unity and gave a chance to the British to rule effortlessly. The Muslims apprehended that the Hindus would be too overwhelming a majority to give the Muslims their due rights. On the other hand, the Hindus were against the weightage and the special safe guards to be given to the Muslims. Thus communal riots broke out and Gandhi went on his historic twenty-one day fast. According to Manmath Nath Das, "the root cause of the idea for Pakistan lay in a fear psychosis of the upper class Muslim elite which feared Hindu domination over a Muslim minority at the end of the British rule. This fear became the seed of separatist tendencies, and with the system of separate electorate injected into Indian constitutional experiments, the rift between two communities developed rapidly." (Partition and Independence, Das, 59)

Jinnah resigned from Congress because it was endorsing Gandhi's campaign. He left all positions in Congress and became an ardent antagonist. But he faced challenges by his own people inside his party. Jinnah, though he believed that separate electorates, based on religion was necessary to ensure that Muslims had a voice in the government, was willing to compromise on this point, but talks between the two parties failed. His mediatory role was increasingly taken over by Mian Fazl-i-Husain, the Punjabi Muslim leader whose strong provincial powerbase and membership of the Viceroy's Executive Council gave him much greater authority in negotiating on behalf of the Muslims. The Muslims from Punjab did not support Jinnah as their representative. So upset with all this, Jinnah spent the years 1930-1935 in London. Jinnah was the "permanent president of the League from 1919 to 1930. He was also sessional president in 1916, 1920, and from 1924 until his death in 1948." (Sole Spokesman, Jalal, 36).

The Indian Muslims urged Jinnah to come back and take up the leadership of Muslim League. However, it was not these appeals and pleads that forced Jinnah for homecoming but rather the 1935 Government of India Act in which he saw an opportunity to recover his former power and impact. The differences between the Hindus and Muslims were widening. When the country was fighting for freedom a large group of communal Muslims were preparing for their separate fight with their single-minded demand. The demand for a separate nation was raised by the Muslims like Sir Sayed Ahmed Khan and great poet Mohammad Iqbal. Sir Syed Ahmed declared that "all individuals joining the fold of Islam, together constitute a nation of the Muslims."(Gandhi Vs Jinnah, Hays, 15) The great poet Iqbal also talked about the "formation of a consolidated North-West India Muslim state appears to me to be the final destiny of Muslims."(India's Freedom, Heehs, 158)The indication of a separate Muslim state was caught by some Muslim students in England and their leader Chaudhary Rahmat Ali provided a name Pakistan to the unknown state of the Muslims. The word 'Pakistan' has its origin in the first letters of Punjab Afghan – the North-West Frontier Province – Kashmir and Sind, and the ending 'stan' meaning land. 'Pak' is an Urdu word which means 'spiritually pure', or clean. But the proposal was condemned by Joint Select Committee and even Jinnah. However, the worsening relations between the Hindus and Muslims forced him to rethink it.

The Muslims of Bombay elected Jinnah, though then in London, as their representative to the Central Legislative Assembly in October 1934. The British Parliament's Government of India Act 1935 gave considerable power to India's provinces, with a weak central parliament in New Delhi, which had no authority over such matters as foreign policy, defence, and much of the budget. Full power remained in the hands of the Viceroy who could dissolve legislatures and rule by decree. (Wikipedia) The League half-heartedly accepted the order, though expressing objections and hesitations about the weak parliament. To follow the instructions of the new Act, the Congress, and the Muslim League decided to contest elections separately. The Congress also decided to fight the election, not to cooperate with the government but to reject the new Act in favour of the demands raised by Gandhi at the Second Round Table Conference. The Congress was much better prepared for the provincial elections in 1937. It won in seven out of eleven provinces. The Muslim League won only 109 of the 482 seats reserved for the Muslims. The Congress had contested only 58 seats out of which it won 26 of them. The League failed to win a majority even of the Muslim seats in any of the provinces where members of that faith held a majority. It did win a majority of the Muslim seats in Delhi, but could not form a government anywhere, though it was part of the ruling coalition in Bengal. The Congress and "its allies formed the government even in the North-West Frontier Province (N.W.F.P.), where the League won no seats despite the fact that almost all residents were Muslim". (*Sole spokesman*, Jalal, 15-34)

The elections of 1937 were the turning point for the Indian politics as well as the Muslim League. After the poor performance of the Muslim League in elections, Jinnah for the last time offered to form coalition ministries with the Congress. The efforts were made to form the Government but "the League leaders ultimately refused to accept the terms proposed by the majority party. The Congress leaders "thought a link-up with the League could knock over the British government which had relied so much on those (Hindu-Muslim) troubles. But Jinnah chose to stress the differences" (*Partition Perspectives*, Rao, 12) The leaders of the Congress were also not in the mood to entertain the Muslim League anymore. Overjoyed with the victory, the leaders of Congress failed to recognise the influence of Jinnah, and Nehru declared that "the future contest lay between the British and Congress, and all other parties had no real importance." (*Partition and Independence*, Das, 61) The Muslim League was not alone responsible for the communal tension that prevailed in India but some Congress men were equally responsible for it. *Bande Matram* anthem was proclaimed by the Congress as their official anthem, but the Muslim League condemned it by saying that it hurt Muslims as it was anti-Islamic. The Congress leaders "failed to rectify the situation fully; they did drop all but the first two stanzas for Congress use in 1939 partially because of the pressure of a section of Congress-men."*(Partition Perspectives*, Rao, 13) These instances showed that the provincial Congress governments neither recognized the difficulties faced by the Muslims nor tolerated their Muslim populations' cultural and religious sensibilities. The Muslim League took advantage of the Congress blunders and from 1939 it did substantially hard work to increase its influence, especially in Muslim-Majority regions where the Congress had won maximum seats. The Muslim League raised its voice by saying that only it could take care of the Muslims, which received a decent response and the demand for Pakistan increased.

The shadow of the Second World War fell on the national struggle and it gave a chance to the Muslim League to fulfil its demand for a separate state. The war increased the need for the Muslim League in front of the British Empire because the British government wanted Indian cooperation; and the Congress did not agree to it. It is not the Congress had no sympathy for the British who were involved in this war between Fascism and Democracy. But to lend support, it wanted from the British Government a clarification about its attitude to democracy and Imperialism. To see the uncooperative conduct of the Congress, Jinnah was asked to see the Viceroy, Lord Linlithgow, on an equal footing with Gandhi. Which, Jinnah later stated, "After the war began ... I was treated on the same basis as Mr. Gandhi. I was wonderstruck why I was promoted and given a place side by side with Mr. Gandhi."(*Jinnah,* Singh, 264)The Viceroy accepted the Muslim League as the voice of the Indian Muslim and labelled the Congress as a Hindu organisation. The separatist tendencies raised their head effectively and the preparations were made for the serious demand of the partition at the annual session of the Muslim League's session at Lahore on 24th March 1940. The Lahore resolution shocked the entire country as it contained the theory of two nations in the Indian sub-continent. The promulgation of the Muslim League broadened the fissure between the Hindus and the Muslims. For Muslims, Pakistan seemed "to the rank and file of Muslims as an escape from Hindu oppression and exploitation. The rich Muslims saw a promise in it, a rare opportunity to make fortunes without the fierce competition of the Hindu mercantile community." (*Partition Perspectives,* Rao, 14) On the Congress side, they adopted a strategy by which India would be declared independent before it could help the British in their war against Fascism. A difference of opinion ensued between the Congress and Subhash Chandra Bose over this issue. Germany had begun to win major victories in the war and Britain was on the verge of ruin. Then the Congress, with its faith in Democracy, expressed its eagerness to join the British in the war if only they agreed to form a Provisional National Government in the centre. But the British Government did not concede even that, whereupon the Congress launched once again the Civil Disobedience Movement in October 1940.

The political environment of India had been changing drastically because the demand for Pakistan dominated the political discussions and opinions. On the British side, they had by now many more reverses in the war and Indian help for them became essential. Therefore, in March 1941, Sir Stafford Cripps had been sent by Churchill "to offer India self-government in return for wartime support went even further to meet Jinnah's demands and conceded in theory the future partition of India." (history)The proposal was rejected by both, the Congress and the Muslim League. The Muslim League overruled it by saying that it did not fulfil the demand for a separate state for the Muslims. The Congress followed the failed Cripps Mission by demanding that the British immediately leave India in August 1942 and launthe ched 'Quit India' movement. The British promptly arrested Gandhi the and major leaders of the Congress and imprisoned them for the remainder of the war. The people, all leaderless, got furious and turned violent in reaction to this, cutting telegraph wires, damaging railway tracks and destroying other government property. The Government had also taken violent repressive measures, going to the extent of using machine guns etc. On the other side, Jinnah wanted to take maximum benefit of the situation so he concentrated on consolidating the Muslim League's position. He planned to move against his rivals in the Punjab who stood in the way of Pakistan. Till that time, the Muslim League's strength was provinces when the Lahore resolution was passed but by 1942 it conquered the hearts of maximum Muslims from middle and lower class. To follow the pattern of Congress and "encouraged by its growing strength the Muslim League adopted a new slogan in 1943 'Divide and Quit'." *(Partition Perspectives,*Rao,15) Raja Gopalachari, the Congress leader of Madras, tried to break the communal tension but failed to agree with both the parties on the same point. In 1944, Jinnah and Gandhi met to talk over the problem which could not be resolved. Jinnah insisted on Pakistan being conceded prior to the British departure but for Gandhi "today there is neither Pakistan nor Hindustan, it is Englistan. So I say to all India, let us first convert it to the original Hindustan and then adjust all rival claims."(*Partition and Independence,* Das, 61)Liaquat and the Congress leader Bhulabhai Desai met before Simla conference and decided to form an interim government at the centre within "the present constitutional framework and appoint all the members of the Executive

Council, all of whom, except the governor-general and the commander-in-chief, should be Indian. Also, that there was to be parity between the Hindus and Muslims in the Executive council."(*Jinnah,* Singh, 327) Bhulabhai Desai prepared a draft and had shown to Gandhi in which he made some amendments. Later two copies of draft were prepared. Bhulabhai and Liaquat Ali signed it which later came to be known as the Desai-Liaquat-Ali Pact which clearly indicates "that Jinnah must have been consulted by Liaquat Ali Khan before agreeing to sign."(*Jinnah,* Singh, 328) When the Congress leadership was released from prison in June 1945; they disclaimed the agreement and censured Desai for acting without proper authority.

To cope with the situation, Lord Wavel held a conference in Simla in which he invited the leaders of the Muslim League, Congress, Sikhs with Scheduled Caste and other groups. The aim of the conference was to form an Interim government. It reached a probable agreement for the self-rule of India that provided separate representation to Muslims and reduced majority powers for both communities in their majority regions. The conference started with a note of optimism but failed because of the uncooperative conduct and demands of Jinnah and the Muslim League. He "claimed it his right to nominate all the Muslim members to the supreme executive council. To him, there could now be no place for a nationalist Muslim in India of 1945 and thereafter."(*Partition and Independence,* Das,66) However, Gandhi and other Congress leaders liked it in comparison of Cripps offer. Even Abdul Kalam Azad, the Congress President firmly opposed the unauthorised and groundless demand of Jinnah because being a Muslim, he knew that "a large bloc of Muslims had nothing to do with the league. The

Congress would be betraying its Muslim members if it accepted Jinnah's demand."(*Partition Perspectives,* Rao, 17) This disrupted the conference, and perhaps the last viable opportunity for a united and independent India.

In the British General Election of 1945, the Labour Party came to power. The new labour minister Attlee was then keen on granting freedom to India. Accordingly, election to the central and provincial legislature took place for forming the Constituent body as well as for forming responsible ministries in August 1945. The Muslim League declared that they would campaign on a single issue, Pakistan. In December 1945, the League won every seat reserved for Muslims in the elections for the Constituent Assembly of India. The picture had been changed when the Muslim League took 75% of Muslim votes and performed much better than 1937. According to his biographer Bolitho, "This was Jinnah's glorious hour: his arduous political campaigns, his robust beliefs and claims, were at last justified."(Jinnah: Creator, Bolitho,158)The Congress too performed respectably in the election. It dominated the central part of India. The Muslim League succeeded in establishing ministries in Bengal and Sind and in Punjab the coalition of Unionists, Akali Sikhs and the Congress took place. The results of the central elections were not different from the former results. The Muslim League won the Muslim votes whereas the other communities trusted in the Congress.

In March 1946, a British Mission consisting of three members of the British cabinet, included Cripps and Pethick-Lawrence came to India to seek an agreement on the constitutional issue. The British in May released a plan for united India in which all the princely and the British Provinces were included. The Cabinet Mission rejected the idea of Pakistan as it had not solved any purpose or complications regarding religion. The communal difficulties had not changed, besides it the other matters such as defence, external relations and communications would be created. But to meet the demand of the Muslims, the Cabinet Mission granted complete autonomy to the various provinces. Sensitive matters such as defense, external relations, transportation, and communications would be handled by the central authority. The Cabinet Mission had opened an option of leaving or joining for the provinces with the union. The Mission also decided to form an interim government with representation of the Congress and the League but it was not decided that how many members of both the parties it would have in the interim government. The important and essential part of the discussion was that the plan was liked by both parties and a hope of united India revived. The hope was shattered completely on 10th July, 1946 when Nehru answered to one of the questions of a journalist that "the Congress would enter the constituent assembly unfettered by agreements and was free to meet all situations as they arose. The Muslim League, it was evident, accepted the plan only under duress. The statement outraged Jinnah and he replied, "This would mean that the minorities would be placed at the mercy of the majority." (*Partition Perspectives,* Rao, 18)

The ultimate result of this was that the partition of the country into two sovereign states was declared on 15 August, 1947 with communal riots breaking out throughout the country. Ian A. Talbot remarked,

"In the constitutional negotiations which followed the elections Jinnah made full use of his strengthened position. His success was greatly assisted by the continued blunders of the Congress leaders. Their greatest mistake occurred in June 1946, when they rejected the Cabinet Mission's proposals for a federal solution to India's communal problem, after Jinnah and the Muslim League had already reluctantly accepted it. Although Jinnah seemed prepared to agree to less than a fully sovereign Pakistan, provided Muslim interests were safeguarded, the Congress leadership appeared intent on hastening its emergence through its own errors. Once the Cabinet Mission had failed, the partition of India became virtually inevitable." (historytoday.com)

The result of the election also became the reason of the partition to some extent. Out of 296 seats, the Congress won all the general seats except nine and the Muslim League won all the Muslims seats except five. The concluding year of the British rule was not acceptable to Jinnah because Jinnah and the Muslim League knew that the Congress would never agree on the partition, if it came in power. To reject the Cabinet Mission plan and to show his anger at the British invitation to Nehru in August 1946 to form an Interim Government, the Muslim League was ready to protest against it through direct action. The Muslim League called upon the Muslims throughout the country and observed 16th August as 'Direct Action Day' in which they showed their anger and strength by taking violent steps like murders, rape, looting etc. The communal frenzy of the Great Calcutta Killing was also spread out in other parts of the country like

Noakhali and Tripura where the Muslims were in the majority. The Hindus were also irritated with this act of the Muslim League. So, in venegence, the Hindus of Bihar also attacked the local Muslims of the area. By the end of the summer, India appeared on the brink of a civil war. Gandhi 'the father of the nation' was treading on the solitary paths of riot-torn interior villages of the country.

Jinnah did not take part in the Interim Government and also refused to accept the leadership of Nehru. In February 1947, the historic announcement came when Attlee declared that the 'definite intention' of the government was to hand over power of the country 'into responsible Indian hands by a date not later than June 1948' and soon Lord Wavell was replaced by Lord Louis Mountbatten. The directives and guidelines were given to Mountbatten to work for united India. In the tense months of negotiations which followed, Jinnah appeared even grimmer and more determined than usual. The leaders of the Congress as well as Akali Dal were strictly opposed to the partition. To understand the situation, Mountbatten held six meetings with Jinnah. The former had advised Jinnah to follow the Cabinet Mission plan but the latter rejected it by saying that India had passed beyond that stage of any such solution and there was only one "—a speedy 'surgical operation'. Otherwise, he warned, 'India would perish.' When Mountbatten was concerned about the bloodshed and violence Jinnah reassured him that once his 'surgical operation' took place, trouble would cease and India's two halves would live in harmony and happiness." (*Partition Perspectives,* Rao, 21) Mountbatten was well aware of the fact that among all the leaders it was difficult to tackle Jinnah because he was very rigid and entirely contrary to the Congress at the matter of united India. The partition became a reality and it clearly showed the helplessness and failure of the Indian leaders as well as the Muslim League because Indian leaders failed to protect united India and the Muslim League interested in forming faced defeat Pakistan.

> "It was after all a 'truncated' or 'moth-eaten' Pakistan... it represented a betrayal of the Muslim League by the colonial rulers. History is likely to record that as between...nationalism and Muslim communalism, the latter was the bigger loser in terms of the achievement of their objectives, the materialization of their concepts and the long-term viability of their gains." (*Communalism..,* Chandra, 293)

The part played by Mountbatten was significant in shaping the destiny of the nation. He agreed with Nehru and other Congress leaders on the partition and after that talked to Gandhi who was not ready for the partition and announced that it happened 'over his dead body'. Mountbatten very cleverly and intelligently handled Jinnah who had alone been a great pressure for all the Congress leaders. Lord Mountbatten carried out the final complex arrangements with lightning speed. The boundary Commission was set up and Sir Cyril Radcliffe, the chairman of the boundary Commission divided the country geographically while Jinnah divided it on religion basis. The provinces selected for Pakistan were North-West Frontier Province, West Punjab, Baluchistan and Sind. India and Pakistan received their freedom on August 14th and 15th, 1947. The partition was declared, and Nehru gave his memorable speech as the first Prime Minister of India at the Special Constituent Assembly Session in Delhi. That same day violent communal riots broke out in Punjab and spread in other parts of the country. They continued until November by which time around 200,000 people had died and five-and-a-half million had been made homeless. The freedom came with the partition and the partition came with the riots which shook the entire sub-continent. It clearly revealed the role of the British and their unjust behaviour towards the sub-continent. Bipin Chandra remarked,

> "The political settlement of 1947 revealed that British commitment was neither to the principle of the protection of minorities nor to Muslims nor even to Muslim communalism. Their policy towards communalism was geared to serving their own political ends. All the promises and pledges to protect the rights of the minorities were at that stage forgotten. No safeguards were provided for the millions of Hindus in Pakistan and Muslims in India." - (*Communalism..*, Chandra, 292)

The enormous inflow of refugees added to the problems which the Pakistan Constituent Assembly already faced. The liability fell on Jinnah because besides being Governor-General, he also acted as President of the Constituent Assembly and was the final authority in the Muslim League matters. Because of political burden his health became a major problem for him as he suffered from tuberculosis since 1930. During the last days of his life he showed some improvement but following an attack of influenza and bronchitis, complications set in. On 11 September, 1948, Jinnah died peacefully in Karachi just over a year after Pakistan's formation. On his death Nehru specified, "He succeeded in his quest and gained his objective, but at what a cost and with what a difference from what he had imagined." (*Jinnah,* Singh, 476)

Several critics have claimed that if Jinnah had lived longer, Pakistan would not have suffered from the political insecurity since independence. The ideology which the Muslim League followed affected the political stability of Pakistan. It actively mixed religion with politics. Besides Muslim League supported landlord sections in the Muslim majority area before independence. But after the independence and the formation of Pakistan, the enmity among these landlords revived. These reasons were responsible for the continuance deterioration in popularity of the Muslim League. The Muslim League adopted communal politics before partition but later Jinnah, after the formation of Pakistan, made it very clear that there would be no discrimination on the basis of religion, caste or creed. During an inauguration of the constituent assembly of Pakistan, he firmly declared that,

> "You may belong to any religion or caste or creed –that has nothing to do with the business of the state …We are starting with this fundamental principle, that we are all citizens of one state..." He elaborated that a citizen of Pakistan "no matter to what community he belongs, no matter what is his colour, caste or creed is first, second and last a citizen of this state with equal rights, privileges and obligations...." He further added without any reservation: "In course of time all these angularities of the, majority and minority communities… will vanish." (*The Man Who Divided India:* Rafiq Zakaria, 161)

The above statement of Jinnah clears his intention regarding Pakistan which was undeniably different from his arguments before the partition. The Muslim League propagated that the new state of the Muslims would be governed according to Islamic and Quranic laws but the speech of Jinnah was different from his saying. The formation of Pakistan was based absolutely on the interest of the Muslims as Jinnah demanded a separate state for the Muslims only. But it is said that it was initiated by Sir Syed Ahmad Khan though according to Rafiq that was because he did not want the British to target Muslims once again as they had done earlier after the revolt of 1857. Otherwise, he considered the Hindus and the Muslims as two eyes of India, if one was hurt; the other was bound to be affected. One more instance was given by Zakaria which proved how Jinnah manipulated things to fulfil his own vested interests.

The Muslim historians solely blamed Jinnah for the partition of India. The leaders of the Muslim League left their supporters in India on the mercy of the Hindus. They had landed safely in Pakistan with their family and friends. In fact, from the Muslim point of view, it was the partition of the Muslim community. Before independence, Muslims were divided as communal Muslims and nationalist Muslims and later they were divided as Indian Muslims and Pakistani Muslims. Refugee Muslims in Pakistan are called *Mujahirs* and they are not equally treated as the native Muslims of Pakistan till now. In India, Muslims are treated equally as the Hindus while the Hindus who stayed back in Pakistan after the partition would be treated like prisoners. Sroop Chand Malhi, a Hindu resident of Sindh, says in an interview with JI, "Our temples are being vandalized and women being raped. Atrocities against us are increasing day-by-day. We won't get permanent jobs unless we convert to Islam. In Pakistan, we are subject to persecution and have to live our daily lives in fear." (Report of Jinnah Institute) The partition of the country dismembered the once united Muslim and the Hindu community and destroyed their historical bond.

Works Cited

Bolitho, Hector.*Jinnah: Creator of Pakistan*, London: John Murray, 1954.

Chandra, Bipin. *Communalism in Modern India,* New Delhi: Har Anand Publication.

Das, Manmath Nath. Partition and Independence of India. New Delhi: Vision Books, 1982.

Hays, Merrian Allen (Ed).Gandhi Vs Jinnah: The Debate Over the Partition, Calcutta: Minerva Associates, 1980.

Heehs, Peter. India's Freedom Struggle (1857-1947). Delhi: Oxford University Press, 1988.

Jalal, Ayesha. The Sole Spokesman: Jinnah, the Muslim League and the Demand for Pakistan (paperback Ed.) Cambridge: Cambridge University Press, 1994.

JI interview with Sroop Chand Malhi, 4 March 2011www.jinnah-institute.org/images/stories/jinnah_minority_report

Rao, Pala Prasada, "An Historical Perspectives of Partition"*India Pakistan: Partition Perspectives in Indo-English Novels.* New Delhi: Discovering Publishing House, 2004.

Singh, Jaswant. *Jinnah: India—Partition—Independence*, Oxford: Oxford University Press, 2009.

Zakaria, Rafiq. *The Man Who Divided India: An Insight into Jinnah's Leadership and its Aftermath.* Mumbai: Popular Prakashan, 2001.

http://en.wikipedia.org/wiki/Muhammad_Ali_Jinnah

www.historytoday.com/ian-talbot/jinnah-and-making-pakistan

HISTORICAL PERSPECTIVE ON THE THEME OF THE PARTITION

The novel is a world populated by people and it builds itself on ideas and knowledge. Fiction is characterized by its obsession with history. It tries to unearth perspectives which are unnoticed or hidden till now under the layers of past. To expose the character of the historical periods, the novelists select the typical man of that age whose life is shaped by the world-historical figures and contemporary society.

The ultimate subject of the historical novel is man in history, or human life conceived as historical life. In several of its greatest examples, the historical novel attains the status of a modern epic in its view of the tragic limits and comic possibilities of man's historical life. (*The English Historical..,* Fleishman, 15)

These historical novels reveal how the Indians in the past could stand unitedly against the foreign invaders, and emphasis is made on the need for unity among the Indians of different religions or regions. The aim of these novelists is to elicit the feeling of nationalism and an awareness of the political situation among contemporaries.

The event of the partition is of national importance with bitter experiences. A historical perspective of the partition is indispensable as the novels have been cast against this backdrop. A number of novels in the Indian sub-continent have been written on the theme of the Partition of India. While some creations depict the massacres during the refugee migration, others concentrate on the aftermath of the partition in terms of difficulties faced by the refugees on both sides of the border. These novels are an innovative effort to make sense of one of the worst extermination in human memory. The brutal incident of the partition was a traumatic experience for those who bore butchery and massacre of the political turmoil in their personal lives. This unforgettable historical episode has been captured by novelists like Khuswant Singh's *Train to Pakistan*, Balwant Singh Anand's *Cruel Interlude*, R. K. Narayan's *Waiting for Mahatma*, Malgaonkar's *Distant Drum*, and *A Bend in the Ganges*, Padmini Sengupta's *Red Hibiscus*, B.Rajan's *The Dark Dancer*, H. S. Gill's *Ashes and Petals* Raj Gill's *The Rape*, Gurucharan Das's *A Fine Family*, Salman Rushdie's *Midnight Children*, Sharf Mukaddam's *When Freedom Came*, K. A. Abba's *The World My Village*, Mahmud Sipra's *Pawn to the King Three*, N. N. Saxena's *Ties—Thick and Thin*, Nina Sibal's *Yatra*, Shashi Tharoor's *The Great Indian Novel*, Amitav Ghosh's *The Shadow Lines*, Chaman Nahal's *Azadi*, Attia Hosain's *Sunlight on a broken Column* and Bapsi Sidhwa's *Ice-Candy Man*. Apart from the analysis of major Indian novels in English on partition, this study also proposes to give a critical survey of the other novels following the partition narratives.

The partition of India and the associated bloody riots have inspired many creative minds in India and Pakistan to create literary depictions of this event. The ghastly tragedies of the Partition have been a major theme with fiction writers in Indo-Anglian writing. The dismay and shock of brutal violence have lured Indian writers. These novelists consider the partition as a collective trauma and outline the different ways in which the event has been remembered. The writers have expressed their revulsion against the partition. The works on the partition belong to different decades in terms of creation and highlight effectively the trauma. The suffering and pain of the partition dawdles in the realization of many writers. They deal with the heinousness of the event by deploying the images of rape, violence and destruction.

The literature on the partition has concentrated on the political course of action that led to the establishment of Pakistan and the associated violence. The first novel written on the theme of the partition in Indian English literature is Khushwant's Singh *Train to Pakistan* (1956). This is Khushwant Singh's absolute attainment on many levels and reveals that he is an accomplished writer. The deeply moving and award-winning novel *Train to Pakistan* is the study of social and cultural milieu of Punjab and its people. It is based on the events just prior to the partition. As Arthur Lal puts it in an introduction to this book:

> "Its intrinsic qualities as a fine novel grip the reader. Throughout, the action sweeps one along. The characters are vivid and highly credible, and Khuswant Singh keeps them going magnificently on two levels: in their quotidian matrix compounded of their passions of love and revenge, their tremendous sense of belonging to a village community, and their insolence and heroism; and

then again on the wide stage set by the tornado that breaks on their lives in the shape of the cataclysmic events of the partition of India in 1947." (Train to..., Singh, Introduction)

Train to Pakistan was first published under the title Mano Majra. The novel is a moving narrative of the partition. It is an admirable work of fiction but very close to reality in terms of the scenes that are created. The story has a disheartening tone that touches the core of the heart. It presents the observations of common people on the political condition of that time. On one hand, the novel succeeds in asserting the value and dignity of a man's sacrifice for his beloved, and on other hand, it reflects various gruesome and explicit accounts of death, torture, and rape in India. In the same way, Chaman Nahal treats the same kind of inhumanity in his novel *Azadi*. Both the novelists have criticised the leaders and the British as the sole reason of the partition. Singh presents Mano Majra as a contented and tranquil village in comparison to the other villages in the country which are under the influence of communalism. He paints a vivid picture of an ideal village where people of different religion believe in the principles of love and brotherhood and are ignorant about the communal tension, but the outsiders spread the virus of communal riots in the village. The novel depicts how religion is exploited by many for serving their own purpose. Naive and innocent people are used by them to multiply the communal tension. But some well-wishers of these innocent people come to their rescue. As M.K. Naik rightly observes, "the impact of partition on a small village on the Indo-Pakistan border is shown here with pitiless realism of description and the swift tempo of the narrative carries the reader along." (*History of,* Naik, 220)

Being a believer of humanism, Singh has faith in the goodness of man during the crisis of man. Khushwant Singh describes the political atmosphere with perceptive sarcasm. A train load of massacred men; women and children give a realistic portrayal of the partition turmoil. A humanistic concern echoes in the novel. The writer has presented reality through symbols and images. The novelist has given weightage to nature which provides a positive influence on the novel. The novel has some elements of humour which enrich the entire effect of the story.

Riots may be caused by a family situation but are aggravated in an atmosphere of fear and suspicion. It is during the riots that man's rationality takes a complete holiday and his savagery comes out with full vigour and force. H.S. Gill's *Ashes and Petals* (1975) records the gruesome event of the partition that consumed Northern India in 1947. It throws light on the repercussion of partition which quivers not only India but the whole world. The author has given a pathetic picture of the bestial horrors enacted on the Indo-Pakistan border during the days of 1947. It is a story of the cultural and political impression of India at the time of the partition. The novel begins with the gory details of the Partition. The locale of the novel takes place around Punjab and Meerut. It acquaints us with the petty politicians who have exploited the tragic occurrence for their own advantage with no consideration for the harm that they are causing to their country by their reprehensible deeds. *Ashes and Petals* is a novel about a young man, Ajit Singh a cavalry officer ties the knot with a Muslim girl notwithstanding the ongoing Muslim Sikh riots. The novel reflects the gruesome aspect of the Partition and the homicide of one's own women folk, in order to save their honour. The book reflects the violence, rape, abduction, communal riots, the brutal slaughter, and uprooted people as the outcome of the partition. The novel marks very clearly the massacre of passengers of train coming and going to Pakistan, their twinge, agony and trauma. The opening chapter of the novel 'The train' renders the dismay, terror, slaughter of the Hindus and Sikhs on their way to India. The train is a powerful symbol in the novel which is the cause behind the loss of humanistic values. The author strongly gives a picture of the grim impact of the train disaster on the mind of the old Risaldar Santa Singh. When the train is attacked by Muslim hooligans, Risaldar Santa Singh shoots his fourteen-years-old grand- daughter, Baljeeto in order to save her from shame and dishonour. Her seven-years-old brother Ajit, sits through the act as a silent witness. Like Chaman Nahal and Khushwant Singh Gill has also hinted towards the inefficiency and mismanagement of government of both the countries in controlling and suppressing the riots. The novelist clarifies the role of politics in the lives of the common man which intimidate them to admit the inevitable. Like *Azadi, Ashes and Petals* also spans the post- independence days. Gill also portrays the realistic picture of the filthy refugee camps. The focus of the novel is to show the disappearance of love, trust, harmony and peace after the partition. *Ashes and Petals* conveys the message of communal love and its victory over hate through the relationship of Ajit and his beloved Salma. Without the blessings of his father, Ajit marries Salma. The novel reflects the ray of hope of reunion of two different communities through Ajit and Salma's marriage. Although it is condemned by many people but Ajit replies, "before partition weren't we all the same? Bapu, you think I have forgotten Baljeeto...But how long will we keep on simmering and poisoning each other's minds? ...I have seen all the blood mingles...." (*Ashes,* Gill, 180) The triumph of love is shown through Salma who wins the love and affection of her father-in-law with a good sense of understanding. With the consent of her father-in-law, she receives the bravery award posthumously for Ajit who dies in the war with Pakistan. It eventually ends with a note of hope for the reconciliation of both the communities.

The riots were the expected consequence of the partition and Raj Gill presents the origin of the riots at some stage during the partition in his novel *The Rape* (1974). It dramatizes the dehumanization of life and the collapse of all human values. The novel provides a glance at one of the most harrowing occurrences not only in the history of the subcontinent but also in human history. Here again, the author has presented human agony and suffering. The love story runs parallel to the theme of the partition. As Khushwant Singh, Raj Gill also closely observes the changing environment of the tiny and calm village. The novel highlights the role of the politicians to pollute the harmonious air of the village. The leaders from the towns and cities reach the small and peaceful village and shed light on the current situation and provoke the villagers to fight against the Muslims. Dalipjit, the protagonist in the novel, is stunned to discover that his Muslim girlfriend, Leila whom he had rescued and given shelter, has been raped by his own father. He is shocked at the immoral and inhuman behaviour of Isher Singh, his father. The novel presents a different picture of human love under the dark shadow of dehumanization during the partition. Leila loves Dalipjit but her love for Dalipjit is like the worship of God. Even Dalipjit clarifies that his relation with Leila is different and more than a mere physical one. The novel portrays the man-woman relationship in its ambiguous and enigmatic forms. In the light of the treatment of the theme of the partition, the spotlight of the novel is to highlight the power-hungry politicians who betray the innocent people in the name of partition. But there is an unusual variance in the novel in comparison to other novels. The protagonist of the novel *The Rape* seems pessimistic about Gandhi's attitude towards the division of the country whereas in other novels like *Azadi* and *Sunlight on a Broken Column* the protagonists have a great respect for Gandhi. The reaction of the common man is shown through the character of Dalipjit's mother:

> "Ashes be on the head of such independence. They burn your houses and they kill your children, and you call it independence. Making people homeless is independence! True it is, in a way……no land, no house, no cattle, no work. All the time is yours and all the world is yours to wonder about." (*Rape*, Gill, 65)

The novelist gives detailed information about the mass killing and the violence. Like Chaman Nahal, Raj Gill also blamed the Pakistan police and government for supporting the fanatic mob against the Hindus. Unlike *Ashes and Petals*, *The Rape* ends with the portrayal of the scene of loot, arson, rape and slaughter in the whole region. The novelist tries to explore the consequences of the partition. Besides political consequences, the novel is filled with the incidents of soul-shattering and the callous impact created by the most gruesome episode.

Balchandra Rajan's *The Dark Dancer* is a memorable work of the partition literature which deals with the theme of the partition at the personal as well as the national level. It is the first novel of Balchandra Rajan who is well-known as a critic of Milton. The novel was translated into numerous European languages and became a Book Society choice. *The Dark Dancer* is a dramatic novel which throws light on the communal massacres at the time of the partition in southern India. It is a deeply tragic, dark and thoughtful. The protagonist of the novel V. S. Krishnan has returned to India after ten years from England. The arrangements of the events in the novel have been presented significantly. The character of Krishnan reflects the culture of two nations. The language of the novel is characterized by intense emotions. The author uses poetic form while telling the story of the novel. The novel is a profound and passionate work which presents Krishnan's alienation with his endeavour to blend conflicting systems of thought. On his return to India he comes to know about the conflict between the Hindus and Muslims over the partition. His marriage is pre-set with Kamala, the perfect Hindu wife. Krishnan is fully satisfied in her company and with his service.

> "The Dark Dancer seems to enact the multiple fissures brought about by the partition in fictional form, invoking traditional cosmologies and the symbolic language of the epic, which ultimately seem inadequate to apprehend the event. Rajan's attempt to develop an allegorical framework, in a move away from descriptive realism, has its limitations as well." (*Witnessing Partition,* Saint, 111)

The changing environment of the nation as well as Krishnan's life is highlighted in the novel. Krishnan's life changes as he is fascinated towards Cynthia, his Cambridge friend. The converting atmosphere of the nation is introduced through Kamalawho goes to Shantihpur to serve in the refugee camps where the Partition is impacted badly and the environment is tyrannical. Kamala begins her life as a nurse when she is deceived by her husband Krishnan. The novelist symbolically presents the importance of tradition and the logic of conventionality in the life of a young man through arranged marriage of Kamala and Krishnan. On the other hand, Rajan focuses on the character of Cynthia as the new spirit of the west who challenges the tradition and custom at every step of her life. When Krishnanapprehends his fault, he too goes to Shantipur. The novelist provides the information about the uprisings and destruction during the partition. Besides it, the author also talks about Gandhi's teaching of truth and non-violence with the help of the character, Kamala. The novel replicates the basic nobility of human nature with optimism and hope. Kamala becomes the victim of the Partition, while attempting to save the life of a Muslim girl. The author does not limit himself only to the personal tragedy of Kamala but also links it with the national tragedy of the Partition.

> "Krishnan perceives the meaning of loss and death at a personal level leading, if not to redemption, to a greater degree of self-realisation. However, the negotiation of collective suffering during the partition is flawed by the tendency to view violence as a spectacle and the uncritical replication of colonial rhetoric on riots." (*Witnessing Partition,* Saint, 112)

The author has presented the partition from a humanistic point of view. However, it is the national catastrophe of the Partition that originates in a personal tragedy in the form of the murder of Kamala. Rajan very successfully and intelligently links the two different aspects.

Difficult Daughters, the first and the recent novel of Manju Kapoor published in 1998, against the backdrop of the partition deals with issues like women, their education and feminine freedom. The novel went on to win the Commonwealth Writers Prize in 1999 for being the best published book in Eurasian Region. The novel deals with the problems of an upper middle-class urban Punjabi family in Amritsar. The novel is "partly travelogue, partly analytical and partly literary history." (*Indian Writing,* Chakravarty, 95)

The novelist communicates with great narrative eloquence on the idea of independence. The setting of the novel is at the time of 1940's in India. The novelist has used efficacious language to expose contemporary society. The novelist analyses the essence of Indian women living in joint families under masculine supremacy. The story of the novel deals with three generations—Kasturi, Virmati and Ida with their principles, perspectives and relationships. The author describes the different types of Indian experience under the British rule and post-colonial times regarding the holocaust of the partition and the complications of women in general as well as in particular. The tone of the novel is gloomy and full of despair. The theme of the novel denotes the Independence desired and obtained by a nation as well as by a woman residing in the same nation at the same time. The novel recounts the story of the protagonist Virmati, born in

Amritsar into an ascetic Punjabi family. It highlights the feeling and perspectives of a young woman, Virmati who does not desire to live her mother's life which revolves around domesticity, marriage and child bearing. The novelist has used symbolic language which expresses the orthodoxy in thoughts and belief. Virmati's history is reassembled in retrospect by her daughter Ida who commences a journey to know her mother's past. The novel talks about the period of the freedom struggle and "while reading the novel one gets the impression that a woman's life is like the life of a nation. Like an investigative journalist Ida struggles to reconstruct her mother's life." (*Indian Writing,*Chakravarty,98) The character of Virmati is illustrated as a new woman of colonial India. Virmati's longing to get education and freedom is compared with India's quest for identity and self-government. The novel is set against the backdrop of changing India. The story of the novel runs parallel. The novel deals with the theme of the partition and life of Virmati simultaneously. Virmati fails to completely live up to her wishes. She goes to study in Lahore discarding the confinement of her mother's world. She dares to cross one patriarchal threshold but gets caught into another and her free spirit is cramped and controlled. In the same way, the national freedom struggle which was against the British rule changed into the Hindu-Muslim enmity which resulted in the partition. Virmati's dreams are influenced by her cousin sister Shakuntala who is an unorthodox and an unconventional woman. Unlike Shakuntala, she is not thoughtful about acquiring education and professional independence but to escape from the pressures of the illicit love relationship she has moved into with her married professor. Virmati marries Professor Harish and becomes his second wife. The novel has some political episodes like the Anti-Pakistan Conference, the Urdu Conference and the All-India Sikh League. The novel strongly reflects the role of women in the form of people whom Virmati meets like Mohini Datta, Sita Rallia, Mary Singh, and Mrs. Leela Mehta, who are all engrossed in the National Movement. The novel throws light on Virmati's state of mind which is indecisive between the demands of her heart and her longing to be a part of the political and intellectual movements of her time. But Virmati is tangled in her own difficulties. She reflects in regret and guilt, "I am not like these women. They are using their minds organizing, participating in conferences, politically active, while my time is being spent in love. Wasting, it." (*Difficult*, Kapoor, 142)

Virmati's married life is absolutely ruined when she is cast out by her family and forced to compete for her share of her husband's love along with his first wife, Ganga. She is forced to adjust herself in her husband's family. In comparison to Virmati, her daughter Ida is clear-headed and strong in her emotions because she dismisses her married life when her husband refuses to take the burden of a child, "I knew Mother, what it was like to have an abortion. Prabhakar had insisted I have one. In denying that incipient little thing in my belly, he sowed the seeds of our break up" (Difficult, Kapoor, 56) Virmati's roommate Swarnalatha is also incapable to force her to take part in the freedom struggle. She asks Virmati to realise the reality of the time. She tells her how plenty of married women are also involved in the freedom movement. But Virmati finds herself shackled in new prisons even as she breaks old ones. The characters of Swarnalatha and Shakuntala, are presented as strong and open-minded women. The novel reflects the mental pain and suffering of a woman through the rebellious character of Virmati. The novel does not speak about the 'difficult daughter' Virmati, Ida and Shakuntala only, but also indicates the several other 'difficult daughters' who have left the restrictions of their household and have involved themselves in the national struggle for independence. These women characters of the novel represent the progressing awareness and responsiveness of the modern Indian woman. There is a quest for identity, brooding and liberalism in these characters. Ultimately Virmati has died an insignificant death though she wins in breaking the age-old restraints of a male-dominated society. But she has paid for her victory a very high cost in the form of her self-respect, mental torture, struggle and the label of the second wife. In the same way, India gains independence from the British rule but at the cost of the partition and communal hatred. The harmonious environment between the Hindus and the Muslim is converted into enmity.

Salman Rushdie's *Midnight's Children* deals with the political turmoil and violence during the first three decades of independence. The novel is divided into three books. Rushdie's most eminent novel, *Midnight's Children* won the Booker Prize and the James Tait Black Memorial Prizein 1981. The novel was later considered the best Booker-winning novel and received the title "Booker of Bookers." In 2003, the novel was listed on the BBC's survey 'The Big Read'. It was also added to the list of Great Books of the 20th Century, published by Penguin Books. *Midnight's Children* is a fictional work of supernatural powers which deals with postmodern literature. The novelist gains the scope for abundant expression in the novel with the skill of magical realism. The characters of the novel are the representation of the culture and customs of India and Pakistan. The protagonist and the narrator of the novel, Saleem is born exactly when India achieved its independence. He was born with telepathic powers and an enormous and constantly dripping nose with an extremely sensitive sense of smell. Not only Saleem, but other children born in India between 12 a.m. and 1 a.m. on that date are imbued with special powers. The progress in the novel is marked by Saleem's life which is analogous to the events leading up to India's Independence and Partition. The novel also deals with the theme of fragmentation. Rushdie succeeds in portraying the character of Saleem as the symbol of the completeness of India. According to S.P. Swain,

"Throughout the novel Saleem's inner life is a function of the historical forces affecting his state. He is, in his own mind, the latent, elusive centre of India's history. His parodying the history of India makes the entire narrative a Historiographic Metafiction. From seeing himself as the centre of the state, he begins to look upon himself as an integral and an inalienable part of the state. His hold upon reality comes `from a view that the reality of the state is fragmented and dispersed in the consciousness of all individuals and not in the consciousness of any one individual." (*Salman,* Mohit, 82)

The story revolves around different places like Kashmir, Agra, Bombay, Lahore and Dhaka. Rushdie depicts the picture of the ancient and contemporary Indian culture. He implements a wide-ranging style to present Indian perspectives in English language. Saleem arranges a conference of all children who have been born in the midnight of the independence. The author highlights the problems and difficulties which India faced during and after the partition through the conference. Saleem uses his telepathic powers as a channel to collect the geographically disparate children to realize the meanings of their powers. He understands the fact that those children who were born closest to the midnight have more powerful gifts than the others. Shiva "of the Knees" and Parvati, called "Parvati-the-witch" are two such examples.

The Shadow Line (1988) is a Sahitya Akademi Award winning novel. It is Amitav Ghosh's second novel, who has overtime secured his place as one of the India's most renowned and eminent authors in English literature. The novel is the reflection of violence that pervades the eastern part of the country. It gives a picture of Hindu-Muslim riots in Bengal in 1964. The riots soon spread to East Pakistan, now known as Bangladesh. Ghosh picks a story that diffuses through the seams of reality and fiction, of time and space, of memories and beliefs. He shows how different cultures and communities are becoming antagonistic to a point of no return. *The author uses the process of* coalescing to disclose the ideas together as time and space and help the narrator to understand his past better. The style of writing is unique and fascinating. It built out of a complicated, interweaving web of memories that hold mirrors of different shades of the same experience. The author has used the language and words in such a way that they are filled with a wealth of meaning. The novel is known for its complicated details of the given time and situation. It is set against the backdrop of historical events like Swadeshi movement, Second World War, Partition of India and Communal riots of 1963-64 in Dhaka and Calcutta. The novel is about a young Indian boy and his life there and, later, in London. It is a story of a middle-class

Indian family based in Calcutta. The storyline is based on the reminiscences of the chief characters of the novel. The narrator is the boy who is sexually attracted to his cousin, Ila, but he prefers to maintain his present friendly relationship. The character of Ila is the showcase of the confusions for the people who live away from their native place and harbour the prejudices they have to face. The boy admires Tridib, a cousin, who falls in love with May, a Londoner who is also a relative. The novel crosses almost seventy years through the memories of people and giving their viewpoint along with his own. Tha'mma, narrator's grandmother is the most apprehended character in the novel. Her character has given a distinct idea of the idealism and the enthusiasm with which the people worked towards nation building just after independence. The book offers a fascinating glimpse of travelling through the character of Tridib who travels the world through his imagination. Ghosh finely tries to open the mythos that boundaries restrict but there are no barriers in imagination. *The Shadow Lines* is a political allegory which urges the need for a syncretic civilization to elude a communal holocaust. Unlike most of the authors, Ghosh gives ample space to the British Price family. The novel provides the message that the partition that human draws between two nations are just transitory and shadowy. *The Shadow Line* is a post-partition novel which outlines the aftershock of the partition by gone trauma which continues to haunt the lives of its victims-- not physically but mentally. It has been closed with the powerful message of the time i.e. the senselessness of creating nation states, the ridiculousness of drawing lines which arbitrarily divide people when their memories remain undivided. Though the major part of the novel is based largely in Kolkata, Dhaka and London, it seems to echo the sentiments of whole of South-east Asia, with lucid overtones of Independence and the pangs of Partition. Ghosh has penned several novels but *The Shadow Lines* undoubtedly remains one of his best.

The independence was accompanied by the political and social strains among the Hindus, Muslims and Sikhs which leads to communal violence. The historic event has produced a vast corpus of literature. All the novelists in his own way have molded and shaped this significant and traumatic national event in some inventive configuration. The influence of the atrocious event was so intense that after many years of the partition, the theme of the partition has been treated with all its atrocities and hideousness by the novelists. With the newly achieved freedom of expression, these authors have expressed in their novels their suppressed rage and potent reaction at the political cataclysms of the country. The novelists are forced to treat the ghastly event because the partition was not only geographical but it was the division of culture, language, traditions, relations, love and friendship. The Partition has provided them only a human world which is only a heartless substitute of a religious community.

Works Cited

Chakarvarty, Joya (Ed). "A Comparative Analysis of Arundhati Roy's The God of Small Things and Manju Kapoor's Difficult Daughters" *Indian Writing in English,* New Delhi: Atlantic Publishers and Distributors, 2003,95.

Fleishman, Avrom. Ed, *The English Historical Novel: Walter Scott to Virginia Woolf,* London: The Johns Hopkins Press, 1971), 15.

Gill, H.S. *Ashes and Petals* , New Delhi: Vikas Publication, 1978, 180.

Gill, Raj.*The Rape* New Delhi: Vikas Publication, 1974, 65.

Kapoor, Manju. *Difficult Daughters,* New Delhi: Penguin, 1988, 142.

Lal, Arthur. Introduction, *Train to Pakistan*, Khuswant Singh New Delhi: Times Books International, 1989.

Naik, M.K. (Ed). *A History of Indian English Literature,* New Delhi: Sahitya Akademi, 1982, 220.

Saint, Tarun. k. (Ed) "Negotiating the effects of Historical Trauma: Novels of the 1940s and 50s" *Witnessing Partition Memory, History, Fiction,* New Delhi: Routledge, 111

Swain, S.P. "Theme of Fragmentation: Rushdie's Midnight's Children", *Salman Rushdie: Critical Essays, Volume 1* Ed. Mohit Kumar Roy& Raman Kundu, New Delhi: Atlantic Publication, 2006, 82-83.

SUNLIGHT ON A BROKEN COLUMN

Indeed, it is a fact of history that the partition has had an unhealthy effect on both the countries, India and Pakistan. The theme of the partition was a source of inspiration for Attia Hosain who was a prominent writer of Indian English literature. Attia Hosain is known as one of the initial female Diaspora writers from the Indian subcontinent. She is among the very few female writers who started their writing profession among the domination of male writers. Her only novel *Sunlight on a Broken Column* demarcates itself from other novels covering the partition theme because it is the first novel which brings out the feminine and Muslim perspectives on the partition of India in Indian English literature. Inspite of being a Muslim, she digs into the critical points of the partition without being biased towards any of the communities.

The novel has its deep foundation on the tragic event which India and Pakistan faced before, during and after independence in the form of the partition. The story of the novel has its root in the partition and also illustrates its aftermath. The novel cautions us against the distinction of religion by men which causes great harm to the country and its people. It introduces us to the feudal system which prevailed during the British rule. The novel represents the city of Lucknow which was one of the great centers of Muslim culture and was also once the stronghold of art, culture, architecture and learning. It also throws light on the colonial encounter between Indians and the British government in the backdrop of Lucknow. The intention of the novelist in writing this novel is to expose the world around her in real and an authentic manner. The book allows the reader to take a look at the life of an upper class cultured Muslim family and a time in history around the Partition.

The novel is authentic and genuine in its presentation. The novelist gives scrupulous details of the plot and the lively portrayal of the characters. The plot of the novel contains the pain and suffering which are caused by the traumatic event of the partition. Hosain shows strength in her writing in presenting the communal divide and riots. Cast in the autobiographical form, the novel is divided into four parts. The first three parts of the novel deal with communal politics and feudal system of the upper-class Muslim society. These three parts reveal the Muslim culture and customs in an elegant manner. The fourth part of the novel highlights the pain and trauma of the partition and its aftermath. Attia Hosain depicts the trauma of the Partition and communal riots through her characters. The narrative technique is pragmatic but the illustrative aspect is very significant. The novel is structured with great intelligence. The use of Urdu words and phrases makes the novel actual and real. The tone of the novel is not blemished by the use of single person narrative technique. Like Bapsi Sidhwa, Hosain also uses only one character to narrate the whole story of the novel whereas Chaman Nahal uses the shifting point of view to describe the whole event of the partition. K.S. Ramamurti rightly remarks, "In Attia Hosain's Su*nlight on a Broken Column,* the partition theme does gain a new meaning because of a particular point of view employed." (*Three Contemporary,* Dhawan, 131)

The title *Sunlight on a Broken Column* is borrowed from T.S. Eliot's 'The Hollow Men'. It has its own historical significance and is heavy with memories. The title reflects a summer of hope and a winter of discontent. The novel deals with the freedom struggle and the partition tragedy. The title reflects the condition of India which represents the broken column after the Partition, but the light symbolizes that there is hope for the broken nation. The novelist assumes an optimistic approach and positive views in the novel. She shows the changes through places, situation and characters. The partition of the country attracted Attia's attention towards the profession of writing. She has written many stories which were published under the name of *Phoenix Fled.* In the novel, she has treated the theme of the partition through the memories of the protagonist, Laila, who endures the pain of the partition. The story of Laila begins from the age of 15 and spans over 20 eventful years. When the novel begins she is fifteen and at the beginning of part second, she is almost nineteen, and towards the end of the novel she is a mother and a widow, "the second half of a century was now two years old."(Sunlight, Attia, 273) Hosain concentrates on the freedom struggle of the country as well as Laila's struggle against the claustrophobia of traditional life. She also focuses on the shrewd policy of the British Government to divide and rule as the major cause of the partition. The action of the novel is revealed through the memories of her disintegrating Taluqdari family.

Attia Hosain achieved eminence and fame for her novel. As a person she had an introvert and a reclusive personality. She grew up between the two worlds, as an onlooker of the external world and retiring in the inside world. She was very close to her culture and her nation and that imparted genuineness and realness to her work as well as manifested her ardent love for her culture and tradition. She could nail down an entire way of life in one sentence. Like the protagonist of her novel, Laila, she did not have much say in family decisions. She was a silent observer and whatever she could not say in public that she expressed in her novel through her characters. Most of the characters in the novel clearly specify some aspects of Hosain's life. The novel constitutes a strong and fascinating cord of emotional longings with social stigmas and political disturbances. It gives details of Muslim culture along with love, marriage and traditional customs which changes with the passage of time. The life of Muslim aristocratic families in the traditional and old living area of Lucknow makes the novel a work of historical realism. The novel records slow but sure loss of power on the part of Laila's family. Laila does not glorify her Muslim past or traditional customs. Family, rebellion, social and political changes are the various areas of focus. Meenakshi Mukherjee rightly remarks, "The narrator being a Muslim, the issues of loyalty, idealism and expediency are brought out with a special significance." (*Twice Born*, Mukherjee, 53)

Set in the background of a feudal, taluqdari, aristocratic Muslim family which represents feudalist officers and zamindars of colonial period, Attia shows her heroine Laila making a departure from tradition and customs. She rejects narrow-mindedness and Epicureanism.The period of the novel is set roughly around 1932 to 1952. Hosain portrays everything in a realistic manner because she herself witnessed the holocaust of the partition. The novel presents the grim and pathetic situation of a feudal Muslim family which belonged to a royal class before and after the partition. The book looks at the partition through the central character Laila, an orphaned daughter of a distinguished Muslim family who is brought up by her orthodox aunts and who keeps purdah. Laila is brought up in an orthodox and conservative environment. Laila's family is not directly harmed by the riots but unfortunately disintegrates due to the partition. The partition bred an atmosphere of distrust between the Hindu and the Muslim communities. This atmosphere of communal disharmony, dreadful animosity and almost tragic suspicion after partition of the country in 1947, is powerfully and rather ironically captured by Attia Hosain in her novel which covers a span of about two decades.

Attia Hosain portrays the political, social and cultural conversion in the Indian Muslim society around partition. She highlights the nationalism and unity of all religions in India during the freedom struggle. The reader is informed about the political activities and the freedom-struggleagainstthe British through Asad and Zahid. The patriotism and loyalty of the young generation of that period is admirable. The College-going youth show their interest in politics and in order to prove their courage, they take part in the joint Hindu-Muslim political procession. Nita and Sita are Hindu girls and Laila's friends while Asad and Kemal are

Muslims. Despite their religious differences, all of them are united for the cause of India. Laila is impressed with the nationalist thoughts of her friend Nita, who has died because of injuries to her brain caused by the blows on her head received during the police lathi charge and Laila feels that, "her death was to me martyrdom". (166) It proves that the Hindus and the Muslims make their efforts together to throw out the British and to protect the tradition and culture of India. Hosain focuses on communal harmony among the Hindus, Muslims and Christians. Mr. Fremantle, a very close friend of Laila's grandfather, who died just after one year of his friend's death requested to "be buried near his friend, and only a simple marble cross distinguished his grave from the others in the family graveyard in the mango grove at Hasanpur." (201) In the same way, Laila's friend Joan, who writes letters to Laila from England once wrote, "It is not possible--at any time, at any age, to forget the place and atmosphere where one was born and brought up. I find myself comparing, and contrasting everything with India; and -- would you believe it? When my parents now talk of 'home' they do not mean England!" (308) The novel discusses the fact that the Muslims are equal sufferer of cruelties and partial behaviour of the British. They also fight with the Hindus against the British in freedom struggle but eventually some of them become the victim of the shrewd policy of divide and rule. Bipin Chandra remarks, "British rule and British policy hold a special responsibility for the growth of communalism in modern India. The British took advantage of it, encouraged it and helped it reach the monstrous proportions that it ultimately did in 1946-47." (*Communalism,* Chandra, 268). The same concept is discussed in Nahal's *Azadi* in Gandhi's speech. The character of Bill Davidson in *Azadi* shows humanity and concern for India and Indians.

Communal violence among the Hindus, the Sikhs and the Muslims were not only due to mutual hatred among the communities for historical and religious reasons but there were some other factors also responsible for the bloodshed. Attia has also pointed out the gradual changes in society as well as in politics, and how the fight of the Indians against the British turned into the conflict between the Hindus and the Muslims. The novelist has recorded an episode of communal hatred and religious riots to define the height of the hatred among people which unfortunately prevails to this day. Both the communities have become scapegoats of political rulers who use innocent people for their own vested interests. During the time of *Muharram*, when;

> "...just outside the big Hanuman temple the top of their *tazia* stuck in the branch of a *peepul* tree...What was to be done? The branch of their sacred tree could not be cut without getting the Hindus angry. But there are many ways of causing mischief. Someone began to blow a conch in the temple, though it was known there was a holy procession outside. Some hot-blooded persons threw stones at the heathen sounds, and then the fighting began. This kind of mischief spreads like a fire in a field of dry grass." (75-76)

Conflict between the different ethnic groups in the country exploded into a civil war. The author insinuates that religion is the root cause of spreading disharmony in society. Hosain openly exposes social differences between the Hindus and Muslims. She has accepted the fact in one of her interviews that even in her closest Hindu friends' homes being Muslim, were not permitted inside their kitchen and near them when they were eating. Infact the character, Saleem in *Sunlight on a Broken Column* states the fact that, "Sita's attitude opened my eyes to the realities of the communal problem, what can you expect from a religion which forbids people to eat and drink together? When even a man's shadow can defile another? How is real friendship or understanding possible?" (197) But Laila has an answer "Ranjit's grandfather did not eat with Babajan, but was his greatest friend." (197) The comment of Rupinderjit Saini is remarkable, "the author keeps close to the historical facts. Though the Hindus and the Muslims had co-existed for a long time; warm relationships at the social level were not really possible." (Journal, Saini, 109) The author not only highlights the effect of the partition but also the causes of the partition. Through these incidents she focuses on the fact that there was no natural tension between the Hindus and Muslims but it was created by the British and some Muslim leaders.

The novelist very skilfully presents the changes in the family as well as in the society. It gives the account of the violence and brutal activities of rioters. She shows the effect of violence in North-Western provinces on the minds of people living in a city like Lucknow. Hosain artistically describes the elegant tradition of Lucknow 'the city of Nawabs' and the changes that are taking place in the city:

> "No one seemed to talk anymore; everyone argued, and not in the graceful tradition of our city where conversation was treated as a fine art, words were loved as mediums of artistic expression, and

verbal battle were enjoyed as much as any delicate, scintillating, sparkling display of pyrotechnic skill. It was as if someone had sneaked in live ammunition among the fireworks. In the thrust and parry there was a desire to inflict wounds." (230)

Everything is observed impartially by the writer. She presents the views of the Muslims who favour the partition and also those who do not want it. The novelist employs certain characters through whom she focuses on the forces of the change that takes place in the society. Slowly and gradually the changes are shown in the family of Laila when, "a new type of person now frequented the house. Fanatic, bearded men and young zealots would come to see Saleem." (230) Attia is honest and truthful about her belief that fanatic Muslims spoil youth like Saleem and Zahid and peace-loving environment of Laila's family is disturbed by the politics based on religion and "every meal at home had become an ordeal as peaceful as a volcanic eruption." (230) This sharply brings outthe undergoing changes in the individual lives as well asin the political situation of the country which somewhere hints at the partition. Hosain observes everything in a realistic manner and the feeling of guilt has been expressed due to the demand for a distinct state by the Muslims that ensued in the brutal incident of the partition.

The author exposes the fact that there was tension not only among the Hindus and Muslims but also among the nationalist Muslims and the communal Muslims. The communal Muslims like Saleem are influenced with the policies of Jinnah and the Muslim League and lay the blame on the Congress as 'anti-Muslim' organization. The character of Saleem shows the gradual changes in the interpretations and philosophy of the young generation of the time which starts thinking on the basis of the religion and not for the country, "you'll find an orthodox Hindu full of prejudice against Muslims." (196) Saleem helps Begum Waheed, the candidate of the Muslim League and Raza Ali during elections but even he does not know when his ideology changes in the company of fanatic Muslims. He forgets his duty and identity as an Indian. He had a healthy outlook on the matter of Hindu-Muslim unity but he has altered his opinion after joining the Muslim League. It is Kemal who reminds Saleem him "How you've changed! You used to say the British encouraged Hindu-Muslim quarrels and drove them apart in order to divide and rule." (254) Saleem starts opposing his father, Uncle Hameed and shows his firm beliefs in the ideologies of the Muslim League and odium for the Congress affirms:

> "I believe the Congress has a strong anti-Muslim element in it against which the Muslims must organize. The danger is great because it is hidden, like an iceberg. When it was just a question of fighting the British the progressive forces were uppermost; but now that power is acquired, now the submerged reactionary elements will surface. Muslims must unite against them." (233)

The statement of Saleem reflects the fact that even an educated Muslim is concerned about his religion and cannot differentiate between right and wrong when there is the question of the religion. The influence of the Muslim League has been shown on the communal Muslims and the Congress Muslims, "are being challenged by the communal nationalist under the Muslim League banner. The politics of the street have invaded the drawing rooms of the sophisticated and even father and son find themselves in opposite camps." (*Explorations,* Dhawan, 25)

Religion is an important factor among fanatic Muslims and even Begum Waheed faces criticism for being out of purdah and following Western culture and manners. Hosain depicts the changing times through the characters like Zahid and Saleem. They show their religious rigidness and interest in Pakistan. These characters are also adequate examples of those Muslims who transform their attitude under the influence of circumstances. In the same way, Zahid, Laila's distant relative and also a student, gives glimpses of the young cohort of his time and kind of thinking, "these people use religion to get rid of their hysteria. They distort historical facts thirteen hundred years old, and divide us when Muslims need to be united against great dangers." (69) The purpose of the author to present these two characters is to highlight the fact that those who have come under the influence of the Muslim League use the same language to show their religious rigidness. The author has thrown light on the tension between two castes of the Muslims-Shia-Suni. The comment of Zahid is remarkable, "I tell you the Shias blaspheme and all such processions are sinful; those who take them out are worse than idolaters, and are damned." (56) The views of Zahid and Saleem provide the evidences that the seed of the partition has been sown, especially among the young generation, "I hate those who are enemies of Islam no matter whom they may be, and I am prepared to give my life for it." (69)

The statement of Zahid reflects the prevailing tension and rifts between the two major religions- the Hindu and the

Muslim. The characters in this novel are not entirely villainous or merely heroic. The youngsters become conservative and are misled by the fanatic leaders of the Muslims in the name of religion and God. They do not make their identity as an Indian but as a Muslim.

Attia Hosain has remained true to her Indian roots and because of that she impersonates noble-minded, optimistic and courageous characters like Kemal and Asad who are brothers of Saleem and Zahid. Their love, trust and loyalty towards India has not been distorted even after the partition and the mercy killings of the Muslims. Kemal an emotional young man, a nationalist and a true Indian, who loves his country, India from the depth of his heart and does not desire to depart from India feels, "I see my future in the past. I was born here, and generations of my ancestors before me. I am content to die here and be buried with them." (288)

He refuses all the opportunities which he can get in Pakistan just for his love and loyalty towards his country, India and is willing to sacrificeeverything for the sake of national pride. He opts for India even at the cost of facing distrust, insult and hatred of the Hindus, "they tested the mettle of our loyalties and faith at a time when all values were on the boil and spewed the scum of opportunism and falsehood." (302)

Kemal tries to convince Saleem and his wife Nadira to stay back in India though Saleem has no such intentions. Both Saleem and Nadira are hopeful of having better opportunities to improve their financial position in Pakistan but Kemal is not tempted and lured even by the offers of the high positions in Pakistan Government. Through his love and trust, he declares that in spite of being a Muslim, his soul and every cell of his body is for India, "This is my country. I belong to it. I love it. That is all. One does not bargain-----" (287)

He is a man of principles who does not compromise even at the cost of his life. The whole aspect of the idea of the nationality is beautifully brought about by the conversation of Kemal and Saleem. The novel focuses on the two painful options for Indian Muslims that either they desert all their properties and memories and depart for the newly-established Pakistan, or stay in independent India as an underpressure minority threatened by the mass execution. Uncle Hameed like his son, Kemal never believes in the principles of the Muslim League. Uncle Hameed dislikes the views of the Muslims League and strongly opposes it, "this Muslim League in which you are so interested, I have heard it called communal and reactionary by nationalist Muslims." (233)

He knows the fact that the British want to continue their ruling in India and to fulfill their purpose they want to divide people, "you have learned a lot of lessons very quickly, Saleem. I always found it was possible for Hindus and Muslims to work together on a political level and live together in personal friendship." (234) Like Uncle Hameed, many of the Muslims who have shown their trust in Congress face the criticism by the other Muslims. Bruce King comments:

> "In *Sunlight on a Broken Column* quarrels within the family are a mirror of the larger issues facing society; the fragmentation of the family by modernization, colonialism, language, religion, education, land reforms and partition parallels the

end of a class, its culture and Muslim India." (*The Internationalization*, Bruce, King, 34).

In contrast to Uncle Hameed, there is the character of Saleem's mother, Aunt Saira who dislikes Hindus, "Oh dear, there is no question, it would be better to have the British stay on than the Hindus ruling." (234) She neither becomes a good companion for her husband nor for her son, Kemal.

The novelist was impressed and influenced by the ideology of Nehru and Gandhi because she had, "witnessed the time when women went out into the streets who had never left their homes before because Gandhiji said so." (Interview of Attia) Like Attia, Laila is also born and brought up when the freedom struggle under the leadership of Gandhiji is in full swing. Laila and her friends Sita and Nita take to wearing saris with the national flag printed around the borders a coarse hand spun cotton to protest against the British rule and support the movement of 'Swaraj' and 'Swadesi' in which Gandhiji requested to spin their own cloth and wear only Indian cotton. Not only Laila, but Attia herself was part of the Swadesi movement. Reena Mitra opines:

> "Attia Hosain's *Sunlight on a Broken Column* is a coalescence of history and autobiography. The history of the Indian national struggle for independence and the subsequent partition of the country, fraught with violence, besides providing the background to the personal history of Laila the protagonist, underline as well, her own struggle for independence from the claustrophobic conditions of a conservative Muslim family. Laila communicates the psychological crisis in her life

of the novelist who, like Laila, was orphaned earlier in life. The novel obviously, is a work of fictionalized self-representation." (*Critical Response,* Mitra, 23)

Attia started to work for the Congress from the age of 14. She portrays the character of Asad, brother of Zahid and Laila's distant relative as a true patriot who never desires to leave his country when his brother Zahid decides to go to Pakistan. He knows that the policy of the British is to divide and rule and that is what he wants to tell the fanatic Muslims like his brother Zahid, "He has learned the lesson the English teach us, Hate each other—love us."(56)Hosain has delineated the aversion of the Indians for the British in India throughout her novel. Asad has an unwavering faith in the Gandhian principle of non-violence and truth, which does not vibrate even at the death of his brother, Zahid:

"The manner of Zahid's death had been a terrible test for Asad's faith in non-violence. He had accepted it as such, believing that bitterness and retaliation could only breed violence and start a never-ending cycle which was a negation of life; but he was human and it needed a conscious effort of will to restrain his bitterness." (318)

Asad joins the Congress party and wants to prove the power of truth and non-violence. He actively participates in educational, social and political work in Delhi and due to his continuous efforts achieves an important position in the Congress party and "was sent as a delegate to the United Nations." (318)

He is a liberal Muslim who thinks about the future of his country and never loses his confidence in himself and in his country India. But sometimes his helplessness agitates him resulting in frustration and despondency, "I tried to believe that humility is a virtue, but forced humility is degradation."(54) The character of Asad reflects the author's believe in the Gandhian principle of truth and non-violence though Asad is criticized by one of his friends, "his idealism is really ignorance; he has not studied history. Has it ever happened that anyone has given up power so easily?" (102)

But the influence and strength of these methods forced history to change and new records were made. The novelist focuses on Gandhi's strong belief of non-violence. Asad has remained a Gandhian in spirit, in spite of sustaining the loss of Zahid. Like Attia Hosain, Chaman Nahal has also focused on Gandhian principles with the help of his protagonist Lala Kanshi Ram. These characters show the magic of Gandhi on the masses.

The author highlights the difference of opinion and attitude among the brothers, although they belong to the same family. The brothers are divided by the Partition in the novel because they come to represent each side of the battle. Zahid and Saleem have different opinions since they have been influenced by the extremist and fanatic Muslims, "The majority of Hindus have not forgotten or forgiven the Muslims for having ruled over them for hundreds of years. Now they can democratically take revenge. The British have ruled about two hundred years, and see how much they are hated." (234) They prove that the policies of the Congress are fake and to be regarded with suspicion. They demand for a separate nation on the basis of the religion, which is not suitable and rational. But Attia never believes in the partition of the country on religious basis and opposes, "if, I as a Muslim am supposed to be part of a nation, I should be in Arabia. Why I am not there? Why do they [the Arabs] not consider us one of them, if only Islam matters?" (Interview of Attia)

Through her protagonist, Laila, she makes this fact very clear. In contrast to the characters like Saleem and Zahid, the author paints the characters of Kemal and Asad. Kemal is always away from the company of communal Muslims and Muslim League, so he believes in his country "I have to fight for what I believe in." (287) Asad remains steadfast in the support of the principles of truth and non-violence, even when he is criticized by everyone.

The strong political atmosphere of Attia Hosain's family dominates her life, thoughts and her work that reflects in her novel. She has given a graphic and intense picture of the feudal society. Attia herself belonged to a taluqdari family and she has given a detailed description of the relation between landowners and peasants. The novelist illustrates the feudal society with its drawbacks of which her ancestors and elders are proud and uncle Hameed says with conviction and confidence, "I am a part of the feudalism, and proud to be. I shall fight for it. It is my heritage…." (234) The impact of the feudal system has been shown through the character of Aunt Saira who behaves in an aristocratic way because she belongs to a royal, high-class and feudal society where discipline and conduct are the prominent tools, "What can you expect, when a Government is run by people who wear *dhoties* to parties and put their dirty feet up on sofas?" (282)

But after the partition, when the Indian government comes into power, it abolishes the feudal system. There is a spirit of defeatism and dissatisfaction among landowners. People like Uncle Hameed want to fight for their rights and for what they have but they are, "losing battle against new forces that were slowly and inexorably destroying the rights and privileges in which he had believed."(282) Aunt Saira blames her elder son, Kemal, for ruining the ancestral property which was a sign of their royalty and status. Rajashri rightly remarks:

> "The partition in 1947 and the dislocation and its impact on the family and the individual is examined here legal reforms in the period come as a threat to feudal system. Political decision has repercussions on the lives of the people. It results in geographical, economic and psychological dislocations. The novelist presents the role played by the class, religion, economic status, education status and patriarchs in the family. She also presents how the democratic foundation and economic transformations contribute to lessen the hold of feudal religious ideologies." (*Indian Women Writing*, Sathupati Prasanna, 203)

As Attia has adeptly dealt with the theme of the passing away of the traditional culture of the ancestors, a similar subject is discussed in the novel *Twilight in Delhi* by Ahmed Ali, a Pakistani writer. He can be called the pioneer of English literature among the Muslims of the subcontinent. In his novel Ali focuses on the declination and degradation of the Muslim culture in Delhi during British rule. Ahmed Ali's novel presents the pathetic condition of the India's Muslims during the British rule. Like Attia's novel, Ali's novel is also nostalgic. It presents the glorious era of the Moguls and predicts the pending collapse of the Muslim power and glory in India with the ruins of Delhi. The title of Attia's novel *Sunlight on a Broken Column* is replete with optimism and hope for future but the title *Twilight in Delhi* indicates pessimism and dreariness. The theme is about the collapse of the culture, tradition and glory of the Muslims. Ali very skilfully portrays the dreary and dismal picture of the times and life in Delhi at the time of the arrival of the British. In contrast to Ali's novel, Attia's novel presents the end of the feudal system on the departure of the British. Both the novelists have been brought up differently but they have much in common. Both are attached to moderate, diverse traditions of social and cultural life of Delhi and Lucknow. Both are linked to a humanistic world-view which is free of racism, fanaticism and sectarianism. Both are anguished by the Partition of the country which destroyed the civilization and unity of the subcontinent.

The novel Sunlight on a Broken Column contains some valuable social and political credentials. Like Laila, Hosain was also an emotional and considerate woman. She valued her religion and felt pride in her ethnicity and parentage. In the first three parts of her novel, she has given a vivid picture of the Muslim culture and effect of the purdah in which, women have been confined so that they were unable to deal with the outside world. They are kept in seclusion and hardly seen in public. It is expected that they perform their religious and social duties but their providence and decisions depend on the males of the family. The women of this generation do not gain anything from the liberal education of the men as they are denied formal education made available to the men.

Hosain depicts the characters of the obedient yet proud aunts, Aunt Abida and Aunt Majida who perform their duties till the end of their life but the prominent decisions of the family are taken by their father and later their brother, Uncle Hameed. The women continue to carry out their traditionally classified roles and receive education that has perpetuated their secondary status. Aunt Abida dedicates her life in the service of her father and later husband. But the character of Aunt Saira and Zahra has shown a different shade of the Muslim culture.Both of them have been tutored in some basics in English and are later instructed to move out of purdah because of their husbands' professional requirements but the education left them ill equipped to enjoy any kind of economic independence. Attia focuses on the fact that the purdah stands for the duty and responsibility in the Muslim religion but women like Aunt Saira and Zahra change this custom for their own selfish need. They adopt only the changes which are beneficial for them. Laila has an empathetic attitude towards the unfortunate and vulnerable. She shows equal concern, compassion and kindness for the poor and susceptible like Nandi and Saliman, her servants. But she gets the answer of her request for help from her Aunt Abida that, "this is a matter of principle, my child. Life will teach you to subordinate your heart to your mind." (62)

In the introduction of the novel, Anita Desai writes about Hosain:

> "Her greatest strength lies in her ability to draw a rich, full portrait of her society—ignoring none of its many faults and cruelties, and capable of including not only men and women of immense power and privilege but, to an equal extent, the

poor who labored as their servants. Perhaps the most attractive aspect of her writing is the tenderness she shows for those who served her family, an empathy for a class not her own." (Introduction)

The author portrays some female characters to give a glimpse of conservative Muslims who have their own impact in the novel. The purpose of the author to paint these characters is to show that these women do not have their own beliefs and outlook but they are influenced by their home environment. The homely and obedient Zahra is the cousin of Laila and Nadira is her friend and later wife of Saleem. These characters represent the typical Muslim society. These girls are not in purda but they are not liberal in their thinking regarding religion. Nadira is under the influence of her mother, Begum Waheed a candidate of the Muslim League and thinks, "For most Muslims of this sub-continent Pakistan connotes something different from other countries of the world." (289)

She loves Saleem and after the partition, both of them opt for Pakistan because Saleem "agreed with his wife, Nadira that partition of the country was the only solution of all its problem." (282)

The upbringing of Zahra is different from Laila. She is not educated as Laila. She is told to obey her religious and social duties. She behaves like a fanatic Muslim and does not want to listen to anything against her religion. She marries Naseer, who is in Indian Civil Service. After the partition, her husband gets the position of the Secretary in Pakistan Government. She does not feel dismayed at the thought of the partition and accepts it to be for the welfare of the

Muslims. In contrast to these characters, Attia paints the character of Laila who is proud to be a Muslim but never believes in the ideals of the Muslim League. She supports the decision of her cousin Kemal and uncle Hamid and opts for India. Laila is brought up by her Aunt Abida in the teaching of religion and light of tradition. She wishes to inculcate the feelings of duty and responsibility in her. She is the only girl in the family who receives education like the male members of her family and gains financial independence as well. Like the protagonist, Laila, Attia is brought up in the world of tradition as well as modernity. As Laila is allowed school and university education, she develops her own perspectives. Like Laila, Attia was intellectual and brilliant in studies and became "the first woman from a taluqdar's family to graduate-in 1933- from the University of Lucknow." (Introduction) Laila doesn't want to be 'paired off like an animal' as her conservative sister and aunt, so she marries Ameer, against the wishes of her royal and high-class family. Attia Hosain's depiction of Laila shows the progress and modernity of Indian society. As Nadia Ahmad remarks:

> "Laila does not tolerate any type of hypocrisy, whether it is found in feudal, religion, or modernist relations. Noticing the fragmentation of (her) culture and tradition, as she seeks to find a place for herself, she deals with her questions and doubts by working herself into a position that leads to a subtle realization of the spirituality of Islam."
> (Road to Bagdad, Pultar, 204)

The novel symbolically presents the growth of Laila with the growth of the country.In the span of twenty years Laila changes from an orphan girl of fifteen to the widowed mother of a girl of that age, in the same way, India too moves from colonialism to Independence with the loss of old feudal system and privileges. Sarla Palkar remarks:

> "In the first place, one cannot neatly compartmentalize the personal history of Laila from the social or national history—in fact what makes *Sunlight on a Broken Column* a three dimensional novel is the manner in which the personal, the social and national issues keep interacting and reflecting on one another." (Margins of, Jain & Amin, 115)

Attia Hosain witnessed the celebration of independence in the midst of bloody migration from one country to another. People were too doped up in violence to notice what was happening. Communal riots that broke out during the partition were the sign of the collapse of all affable and pleasant relations between the two communities, the Hindus and the Muslims. Communal violence in the train has been touchingly described in the novel through Zahid who is killed in a train tragedy:

> "Full of bright hope and triumph Zahid had boarded the train on that thirteenth day of August which was to take him to the realization of his dreams, on the eve of the birth of the country for which he had lived and worked, when it had reached its destination not a man, woman or child was found alive." (310)

The restlessness, fury, abduction, mutilation, arson and mass violence of both communities during the partition has been presented by Attia:

> "I had known the fear of violence, murder, rape, and mutilation, as hated-blinded revengeful men had streamed over the border closer and closer to that retreat in the hills. Had the silent hills turned suddenly into flaming volcanoes, and the primeval forests released their wild beasts, the terror would not have been greater than waiting with my child for the beasts that had been men." (304)

Being a humanist, she believes in man's indispensable kindness and decency, but the horror-packed partition manifests man's intrinsic capacity for malevolence and immorality.

The novel deals with a young woman's personal crisissetagainstthelargerhistorical background of communal hatred. It is through the bold and immense personalities like Kemal, Asad and Uncle Hameed that Hosain consoles herself and realizes that the entire Muslim community is not accountable for the demand of an astute state; similarly, the entire Hindu community is not to be impugned for the brutal violence of the partition. She proves her conviction through the choices made by the characters of the novel. The Muslims areas are annihilated and scorched by the rioters. Hosain throws light on the graciousness and benignity of Hindus that in spite of the environment of violence, loathing and antagonism for the Muslims, many of the Hindus protect the lives of thousands of Muslims and establish human values. When all around Hindus are killing Muslims mercilessly, at that time Sita and Ranjit, who are Hindus save Laila and she asks Zahara:

> "Where were you, Zahra, when I sat up through the nights, watching village after village set on fire,

each day nearer and nearer... Do you know who saved me and my child? Sita, who took us to her house, in spite of putting her own life in danger with ours. And Ranjit, who came from his village, because he had heard of what was happening in the foothills and was afraid for us. He drove us back, pretending we were his family, risking discovery and death." (304)

A realistic presentation of communal violence and the slaughter of the Muslim families through the heated conversation between Laila and her alter ego of a cousin, Zahra which is symbolic of the painful internecine debate that goes through many Muslim families. The novelist presents the condition of the picture of other side of the border through Zahra and Nadira. Their humanitarian attitude leads to their involvement. The characters are authentic and mirror the anxieties and frustration of the novelist. They face desolate and harsh choices before and after Independence. Deeply and utterly disappointed Hosain criticizes the Muslim leaders not only for provoking communal hatred and anger against the Hindus but also for running away to Pakistan leaving their co-religionists behind at the mercy of the angry Hindus, "where were all their leaders? Safely across the border. The only people left to save them were those very Hindus against whom they had ranted." (304) Hosain is impartial while depicting communal fury. With the description of a refugee, she shows his hatred towards all Muslims for not helping him and calls them "all bloody traitors" (302). Laila reminds Zahra about the meaning of duty and responsibility of the Hindus, "to stop the murderous mob at any cost, even if it meant shooting people of his own religion."(304) and Hosain learnt this responsibility from one of her friends who was Chief Secretary in Uttar Pradesh at the time of the partition and he said to her:

> "Now think about it for a minute. I had to give orders to shoot if there is a riot. I am a Hindu. Where are all those leaders of the Muslims? Where they have gone? When I have to do the shooting on my own, co-religionists? Why are they sitting across the border [in Pakistan] when this is happening? And I have to shoot Hindus." (Introduction)

Hosain communicates the message that the strength of love is stronger than that of hate and abhorrence can be answered by only compassion. The characters like Sita and Ranjit, throw light on the reality that humanity still survives amidst violence and trauma of the partition. But the author seems to ask the question as to what happens to the magic of Gandhian principles of truth and non-violence. Are people really following or understanding the true meaning of Gandhian principles? Or do they are they just accepting it for their convenience. Perhaps they do not understand the meaning and power of Gandhian principles of truth and non-violence.

The narrative perspective of the fourth part of the novel is about the aftermath of the partition. The novel not only describes the pain of the partition of the sub-continent but also the partition within the family. Laila breaks away from all the shackles of rules, customs and tradition when she falls in love with Ameer Hussain, a university lecturer and marries against the desires of her all relatives and elders. The struggle of Laila against the claustrophobic traditions of family life is represented by the freedom struggle of the country. The heart-rending news of Ameer's death in a war shatters her. She is alone with her daughter to face the difficulties of life and the revulsion of the partition. Attia chooses a different ending unlike the traditional novels. Unlike Khuswant Singh, her protagonist, Laila loves Ameer a Muslim boy. Khuswant Singh's hero Jugga loves Nooran a Muslim girl and sacrifices his life to save her.

The narration of the fourth part also provides a striking insight into the mind of an old woman who stands in her deserted house that is the symbol of their royalty and prestige. As an old lady, Laila remembers her lost days in her home 'Ashiyana' which has been shattered after the partition. The novel gives indication of Hosain's endowment for reminiscence and sensitive observation. She introspects the day when her house 'Ashiyana' was sold. Ashiyana is the house where she has spent her childhood and has memories of her relatives. But the partition snatches the memories of her love for Aunt Abida and Hakiman Bua and also the memories of her friendship with Asad and Kemal are lost. Antoinette Burton remarks:

> "The memory of place, and specifically of the physical layout and material culture of home is a common feature of partition narratives—a phenomenon that reminds us of how intimately connected spatial relations are to social relations, as well as of how influential architectural idioms can be of the practice of remembering." (*Dwelling*, Burton, 102)

The author has developed the character of Laila in an ambiguous and complicated manner. Belonging to a conservative Indian Muslim family she grows up amidst strict family traditions and social constraints. However, she experiences the traditional as well as modern atmosphere in her home under the supervision of her grandfather and uncle Hamid though she is unable to break the shackles of convention. She does rebel against the constraints though, in a subdued manner. The novelist illustrates the rebelliousness of Laila against her family and her search for identity. Attia expresses her isolation of life through Laila. After the death of Ameer, Laila experiences the pangs of loneliness in her life. The character of Laila can be compared with Lala Kanshi Ram in Azadi. He also feels isolated after facing several difficulties during the partition.

Hosain deftly expresses the grief of an individual and of the family that suffer the traumatic aftermath of the partition. The only difference in 'Sunlight on a Broken column' when compared to other novels that in the present novel, the protagonist Laila and her family belong to a noble and prosperous background. It is due to this that they are not harmed physically or directly but tortured emotionally and mentally. Attia has proficiently described the mental condition and distress faced by the Muslims. She has given an account of pain and struggle inflicted on Muslims by the corrupt government officers. Muslims has been humiliated and put to constant searches and lengthy cross-examinations. Hosain sarcastically remarks about Kemal, "He was grateful he had not been harassed as so many others had been by petty officials who ordered humiliating searches of houses and lengthy cross-examinations." (278) Kemal has to show the share of Saleem in the property under the law of 'evacuee property' but his mother thinks that the Indian government is deliberately harassing the Muslims and taking away their property, "No government can behave like thieves and robbers." (262) With the main focus on one talqudar Muslim family, the novelist describes the disintegration and fragmentation of families as well as communities, loss of life and material wealth and the despair suffered by so many people which eventually leads to the mass exodus from one new emerging country to the other, from India to Pakistan and vice versa, based on the religion of the refugee. The families of the Muslims, who decide to stay back in India, have endured years of torment and abuses at the hands of the Hindus. Many of the landowners have lost their land, prosperity, name, fame and even their own people. Some of them have lost their mental balance. The agony, bitterness and frustration of the Muslims is reflected in Aunt Saira's question:

> "What right they have to steal what is ours? Will they never be content with how much they rob? Is there no justice? Is this a war with Custodians for enemy property? Did they not consent to the partition themselves? Why treat those people like enemies who went over? Were they not given a free choice? Were they warned they would lose their property, and have their families harassed? If they want to drive out Muslims why not say it like honest men? Sheltering behind the false slogans of a secular state! Hypocrites! Cowards! It is good Saleem has gone away. They will destroy you and all fools like you who have trusted them. The Banias!" (279)

Aunt Saira's reaction shows the anguish of the elite Muslims. This is indicated through Aunt Saira, that those who oppose the idea of the partition are relegated to loneliness and despair. She is in the throes of mid-life crisis which makes her rather difficult to live and understand the reality of the partition and she criticizes Kemal, "he did not care for his traditions or for her; he had sold himself to a Muslim-hating Government" (279) Aunt Saira does not understand what partition has given them. What is the use of it? Who is benefitted by the partition? Even today, they are finding the answers to these Questions. The character of Aunt Saira can be compared with Bibi AmarVati of *Azadi* because she has also lost everything including her son, husband, and property like Aunt Saira. Both the characters are similar in their perspectives regarding people belonging to different religions. They hate them. But after facing all the trauma of the partition, the novelists of both the novels make a strong appeal to abstain from hatred and to follow the policy of love, tolerance and co-existence.

The changing social conditions of the country before and during the partition have been analyzed critically. Hossain spent most of her time in Lucknow when there were healthy and friendly relations between Hindus and Muslims. They celebrated Diwali, Holi and Eid together. Both communities were fighting against the British together but this peaceful environment had infiltrated with politics. Being from a political background, she was aware about the demand of a separate state by some, "pro-British Muslims like Aga-Khan", and a certain class of Muslims who felt that their existence was in danger. These Muslims were trying to resuscitate the Muslim league. The political struggle for independence sharpens along with the ill-fated rise of separatist tendencies tended in Indian politics by the Muslim League and the leaders which resulted in the partition. The last part of the novel reveals the horror and plight of Laila's royal and powerful family and friends. The creation of Pakistan gives the chance to Indian Muslims to migrate and experience a sense of security and freedom. Saleem opts for Pakistan and Kemal decides to stay back in India and both the brothers try to make their point clear as to why they are forced to take such decisions. Both the brothers, have different views but one thing is common between them and that is that they want to protect their family from disintegration, but the time demands the proof of their loyalty. The partition ruins their past, splits their present and reduces the possibility of their bright future. Deeply hurt Attia questions why should a Muslim always give proof of his loyalty? Why do the demands for Pakistan make every Muslim a criminal? The partition of the subcontinent effects the relations of both the countries and, "It was easier for them thereafter to visit the whole wide world than the home which had once been theirs." (289). Laila and her family, though unaffected by communal frenzy were victims of the partition of a country on a purely religious basis. Attia never agrees with Partition. She is inconsolable and forlorn by the disintegration of her family because of the partition.

But the novel projects the ennobling influence of love which brings out the spirit of friendship and tolerance found among some Indians and Muslims. The novelist brings this message through Saleem and his wife Nadira who return to India after two years of stay in Pakistan and is deeply moved to see that both communities have forgotten the bitter memories of the partition. While in Pakistan, he is still considered as an outcast, "he was glad of the feeling of recognized identity in Hasanpur after having lived among strangers who knew him as an individual without a background." (299)Saleem saw his future in Pakistan and left India for his promotion and security is apologetic, "I am glad you are effete enough to forget your political affiliations, to say, 'Welcome, friend' and not 'Go back traitor!"(301)

Even his wife, Nadira, who left India for her 'neo-paradise' Pakistan because she felt that "Pakistan needs us to build it up as a refuge where all Muslims can be safe and free."(288) but she has changed a lot and "her youthful enthusiasm, for an Islamic Renaissance was no longer aggressive" (299) Hosain shows the changes in the individual as well as in society after the partition. She brings out the changes in the common men who are not very much influenced with the nationalistic thoughts, "European and American aesthetes and intellectuals and the 'smart set' ofBombay and Delhi had discovered the art and culture of ancient India simultaneously. It appeared at times that neo-Indians wore their nationalism like fancy dress." (276) According to Anuradha Dingwaney Needham, "Her narrative possesses the potential to dismantle altogether nationalism's might of homogeneous, continuous and essentialist national identity."(*Modern Fiction*, Needham, 107) Like Chaman Nahal, Attia also throws light on the consequences of the partition. Chaman Nahal gives a glimpse of the changes in individual through Lala Kanshi Ram and in the society through the reaction of people on Gandhi's death.

The economic and political backwash of the partition is still being felt. Attia Hosain suffered the pain of the partition of her family as well as her country. The novel brilliantly evokes the trauma of those Muslims who decide to live in India. Attia bore the excruciating pain of the partition and the wounds of the partition did not heal till the end of her life. In the introduction of the novel she writes:

> "Events during and after Partition are to this day very painful to me. And now, in my old age, the strength of my roots is strong; it also causes pain, because it makes one a "stranger" everywhere in the deeper area of one's mind and spirit *except where one was born and brought up."*
> *(Introduction)*

But the novel makes a strong appeal to spurn all abhorrence and hatred and embrace non-violence and love. There is an influential message that nobody should be blamed for this bloody and gory partition, instead we should judge and introspect ourselves. Attia died on January 25 1998 but through her novel, she tries to unveil the hypocrisy behind most religions. She advises people to give up mindless superstitions and pointless rituals. She has tried to motivate people to overcome the problems which they faced during the partition and move forward. Like, Chaman Nahal, Attia also gives the optimistic view to start life afresh through Laila when she feels, "….I was my own prisoner and could release myself." (319) The sentence gives the symbolic meaning that Laila wants to start her life again. Laila desires a life in a society which is open to Western thoughts and progressive attitudes. The novelist has described the atrocities perpetuated by the communities upon each other and feels that this should serve as a lesson to all people so that such horrors are not repeated in history. The novel also cautions us against religious intolerance which spews hatred and brews havoc. According to the novelist, this is the happy sunlight on a broken column of humanism. These views and perspectives of Hosain offer a hope for sanity which is important and relevant to ease the tense relations between India and Pakistan.

Works Cited

Ahmad, Nadia. "Cracking India: Tradition Versus Modernity in Attia Hosain's Sunlight on a Broken Column and Manju Kapoor's Difficult Daughters" *On the Road to Baghdad or Travelling Biculturalism: Theorizing a Bicultural Approach to Contemporary World Fiction.* Ed. Gonul Pultar USA: New Academia Publishing, LLC, 2005.

Burton, Antoinette. "A Girlhood Among Ghosts: House, Home and History in Attia Hosain's Sunlight on a Broken Column" *Dwelling in the Archive: Women Writing House, Home and History in Late Colonial India.* New York: Oxford University Press, 2003.

Chandra Bipin. "The Role of British Policy" *Communalism in Modern India,* rev. ed. New Delhi: Har-Anand Publications, 1984.

Cowasjee, Saroj. "The Partition of Indo-English fiction" *Explorations in ModernIndo-EnglishFiction*Ed. R.K. Dhawan, New Delhi: Bahri, 1982.

Desai, Anita. Introduction, Sunlight on a Broken Column by Attia Hosain, New Delhi: Penguin Group, 1961.

Hosain, Attia *Sunlight on a Broken Column* New Delhi: Penguin Group, 1961, 273. (All the subsequent references given in the parenthesis are from this edition)

King, Bruce. "The End of Imperial England and the Seeds of the New: 1948-1969", *The Internationalization of English Literature.* New York: Oxford University Press, 2004.

Mitra, Reena. 'Indian English Fiction: The Theme of India's Partition' *Critical Response to Literature in English* New Delhi: Atlantic Publishers & Distributers, 2005.

Mukherjee, Meenakshi. *The Twice Born Fiction* New Delhi: Arnold: 1971, 53.

Needham, Anuradha Dingwaney. "Multiple forms of (National) belonging: Attia Hosain's Sunlight on a Broken Column" *Modern Fiction Studies* 39: 1, 1993.

Palkar, Sarla. "Beyond Purdab: Sunlight on a Broken Column", *Margins of Erasure* Ed. Jasbird Jain & Amina Amin New Delhi: Sterling Publisher, 1995.

Ramamurti, K.S. "Azadi—Point of view as Technique," *Three Contemporary Novelist,* Ed. R.K. Dhawan. New Delhi: Classical Publishing Company, 1985.

Saini, Rupinderjit "From Harmony to Holocaust: A Study of Community Relations in the Partition Novel", in Journal of the Inter University Centre for Humanities and Social Sciences Shimla: Rashtrapati Niwas, Nov. 1994.

A BEND IN THE GANGES

The event of the partition has its own national importance and bitter experiences. Some of the important writers seem to have been actual witnesses to this horrid historical event. Manohar Malgaonkar, a Maharastrian novelist was one of those novelists who has presented the theme of the partition in several of novels. *A Bend in the Ganges* (1964) is one of them.

The novel throws light on the darkest part of the history of India. Malgaonkar paints a picture of the holocaust that followed in the wake of the partition of the country. The novelist depicts the violence, bloodshed, racial hatred, looting, abduction and dishonouring of women with precision and exactness. He claimed that the event of the partition was one of the 'bloodiest upheavals' of history. The novel deals with the aspect of political betrayal very convincingly. It presents the political scene of changing India during independence and the partition. Malgaonkar makes a strong indictment of the British. The author exposes the Indians who are hysterically complaining about the British. The novel set during the period just prior to partition and the onset of freedom is a cleverly crafted piece of literature. It is about the violence that disturbs the common people during the partition. The author has shown a detached realism and skill in depicting the brutal incident of the partition which along with the national movement and the war make for superior artistry.

The novel has a wide canvas. It has an enthralling story and well-constructed plot. The presentation of the novel is distinctive and genuine. It is also slightly different from Malgonkar's other novels. The basic symbolism of the title is linked with the theme of the book. Dinesh Chandra observes:

> "The title of the novel is symbolic and suggestive of a trend of thought which experienced a sudden bend in the course of its flow. The Ganges stands for the heart of India. From time immemorial it has been looked upon as the life blood of India. Its flow from west to east is suggestive of the characteristics feature of Indian thought." (*Indian English...*, Gajendra, 138)

The author has a style and keen observant power that recreates reality with its minute shades and vivid colour. The novel is divided into 36 chapters and every chapter has a subtitle. The partition causes one of the great human convulsions of history which is described mainly in the last part of the novel. The writer traces the horror of the partition to emphasise on the social and political condition of India. The novel has the element of great realism and a dynamic theme. This is symbolical in the presentation of the theme. The theme of the novel is traditional and has been praised by readers across the world. The powerful theme of the partition is also introduced by the novelist in another novel 'Distant Drum'. As A.N. Dwivedi remarks:

"Malgonkar's narrative technique is always flawless. In describing an event or in unfolding a plot, he is unquestionably superb. Most of his stories are told in the third person and in the past tense.... Though in *A Bend in the Ganges*, he becomes multifaceted and epical...And as a historian, he does not remain detached and dispassionate. His predilections and preferences are obvious enough and sometimes lead to distortion." (*Perspectives on...*, Naik, 146)

The writer very delicately and sincerely paints the characters according to the plot of the novel. The novel has very real characters set in a time in history which are the last days of the British rule. Independence and the partition are described with uncanny plausibility. The novel *A Bend in the Ganges* is a plot- oriented novel in which the situation leads the characters. The depiction of the characters and events has an extraordinary authenticity. Malgaonkar uses traditional English in the novel. In order to create the picture of the freedom struggle, the author uses some Hindi words like 'Mahatma Gandhi ki jai!' 'shabash' 'Vande Matram'. The novelist exposes the political scenario of that time through the characters of the novel.

Malgaonkar presents the colonial encounter between Indians and the British Government against the backdrop of Punjab which is known for its military history and is always related to Indian history and politics in the novel. Most of Malgonkar's novels are based on the colonial period. The novel deals with the pre-independence India of around 1940s. The novelist shows the impact of the European colonialism in India. Among the other partition novelists,

Malgaonkar has given a detailed picture of the prison of Andaman during the colonial rule with the help of the protagonist, Debi Dayal. He has provided the description, in one of his chapters under the name of 'The View from Debi's Cell'. Malgonkar also throws light on the pitiable condition of the prisoners who are living there amidst inhuman conditions. M. Keith Booker opines:

> "Among other things, he includes a vivid description of a colonial prison that (especially if read through Foucault's understanding of the prison as a microcosm of the modern disciplinary society) can be taken as a commentary on the workings of colonial power. Moreover, Malgonkar's description of this prison includes a strong historical element, which suggests changes in the operation of this prison that parallel historical developments in the Raj as a whole." (*Colonial Power,* Booker, 93)

Colonial rule has played an important role in influencing the situation of inter-dependence between the ruler and the ruled. The colonial encounter between the Indians and the British was coming to a climax on account of the nationalistic consciousness among the Indians. A mixed reaction among Indians towards the British is presented by the novelist accurately with the strange mixture of attitude to the alien rule. The author "mostly takes Englishmen as paragons of honesty and integrity, and occasionally accuses Indians of lack of sincerity and sense of justice." ((*Perspectives on...*, Naik, 146) In the case of India, the author describes the situation in which the British coloniser succeeded in invading the mind of the colonised.

Dewan Bahadur Tekchand, a rich magnate in Lahoreis into ammunition manufacture and Debi Dayal's father is the appropriate example of the colonised mind. His relationship with the British is representative of the relationship between Indians of his class and the English. The character of Tekchand can be compared with Lala Kanshi Ram in *Azadi*. He is also a representative of the colonised mind and under the deep impression of the British. He favours the British rule and their discipline. Both the novelists try to reveal the fact that the British not only ruled over the Indians physically but over their minds also. The mutual relationship between Tekchand and his son Debi Dayal is also ordinary. As it is usual with father and son, they represent two conflicting views. They represent two conflicting views. The author focuses on the hatred of the Indians through Debi, Shafi, Basu and the others who form Hanuman club to fight with the British. But Debi and Shafi have personal reasons to hate the British. The novelist has tried to reveal the mental condition of a young youth like Debi who has seen 'a bull-necked soldier' from the Scottish border who attempted to rape his mother. He is shocked to see the miserable condition of his mother. The thought of rape always haunts his mind. The frustration and anger of Debi towards the British is depicted through his revolutionary activities. The novelist effectively pulls out the pain of Shafi who has lost his father in the Massacre of Jallianwala Bagh and faced the callous and merciless punishment of the British:

> "As a boy of seven, he had been taken to identify the body of his father, flung obscenely on a heap of other bodies, in the enclosure of the Jallianwala Bagh. It was a hot April day in the year 1919, and the dead of Jallianwala had already begun to

smell….and it had taken a long time to discover his father's body….that same evening…..Shafi Usman and his wailing mother had found that….they had to crawl on their bellies because General Dyer had promulgated what was called the crawling order." (*A Bend…*, Malgaonkar, 58-59)

Malgonkar attracts the attention of the readers by his realistic depiction of the merciless and inhuman behaviour of the British. He also focuses on the 'divide and rule' policy of the British through the character of Gian who betrays his fellow Indians for the British.

The novel opens in pre-independent India and ends during the partition. The background of the novel is placed in the region of Punjab especially places like Duriabad and Kerwad. Politics forms the backdrop of the novel and its foreground is occupied by the two central characters—Gian Talwar and Debi Dayal. The novel deals with two remarkable themes—the freedom struggle and the conflict between the Hindus and the Muslims. It depicts the stark political realism and the theme of communal discord which leads the country towards the partition. The activities of a group of terrorists outside Bengal whose leader is Shafi Usman, popularly known as Singh is also presented in the novel. He is the most wanted man in the records of the British authority. This brings in the Hindu-Muslim solidarity strand. The Hindus, Muslims and Sikhs, all are a part of the band of terrorists. The slogan 'Jai Ram!' is coupled with 'Jai Rahim'. The author throws light on their activities to show their unity which is similar to the unity of the society and all religious groups. The revolutionaries are together against the British.

The Hindu revolutionaries are ready to sacrifice their lives for their Sikh and Muslim friends and the Muslim revolutionaries save the life of their fellow revolutionaries at the cost of their own life. But the harmony is to be soon destroyed. The revolutionaries who were fighting against the British are now fighting among themselves. The author is well aware of the social conditions that prevailed during that time. As he has made a comprehensive study of Indian history and politics, he has been able to give a political mould to the novel. The conversation between Shafi and Hafiz provides vital information about the root cause of the problem. The characters of Shafi Usman and Hafiz represent the Muslim population who has hankered for a separate country. Their conversation reveals the fear and thinking of the Muslims who want a separate nation for themselves, "Now we Muslims have to look after ourselves. Organize ourselves before it's too late. Carve out our own country...." (73) Hafiz is a representative of the fanatic Muslims and Shafi represents the nationalist Muslims. In the same way, Attia Hosain exposes the problems between communal Muslims and the nationalist Muslims in her novel *Sunlight on a Broken Column*. Saleem can be compared with Shafi. In the beginning of their novels, both the characters, Saleem and Shafi are true nationalists at heart but the communal Muslims turn them into communal and fanatic Muslims. Both the novelists somewhere, want to highlight the fact that communal Muslims like Hafiz in *A Bend in the Ganges* and Raza Ali in *Sunlight on a Broken Column* are not expressing their own opinions but the motives of Jinnah and the Muslim League. This is clear when Hafiz says:

"We don't want freedom if it means our living here as slaves of the Hindus. If we succeed in driving out the British, it is the Hindus who will inherit power. Then what happens to us? We are heading for a slavery far more degrading... struggling for it. That's what Jinnah is worried aboutwe have to organize ourselves—Muslims against the rest of India, if we are to survive. Organize, not so much to win freedom, but to protect ourselves from being swamped by the Hindus; emasculated, to become a race of serfs in a country ruled by idolaters." (73)

Malgaonkar stresses on the point that the Hindu-Muslim rivalry is not the result of recent times, but it has been the shrewd policy of the British to divide and rule which changes the direction of the freedom struggle and the harmonious environment of the country. Hafiz has succeeded in turning Shafi into a communal Muslim when "he suddenly realized that all those who would be in the club at the time of the raid would be Hindus, there would not be a single Muslim among them." (76) The novelist seems to be suggesting that communal hatred was injected into the minds of Indians in order to disrupt the country's struggle for freedom. The author presents the perspectives of the Muslims as well as the Hindus in order to show the real picture of the society when Basu, one of the terrorists of the group says, "And the ugliest thing it has bred is distrust. No Hindu can trust a Muslim any more, and no Muslim trusts a Hindu. The country is divided." (245) These lines reflect the fear of the violence and the civil war that is imminent during the partition. Not only the Muslim League but even the Hindu Mahasabha is preparing for war:

> "The moment the British quit, there will be civil war in the country, a great slaughter. Every city, every village, every bustee, where the two communities, live side by side, will be the scene of the war. Both sides are preparing for it, the Hindu and the Muslims. The Muslim League and the Hindu Mahasabha are both militant…" (246)

The psychological reason of the Muslims for demanding a separate nation for themselves is hinted by the novelist. The Muslim League alone is not to be blamed for the brutal incident of the partition but some Hindus are also accountable for that. Although Malgaonkar provides some incidents to prove the Hindu-Muslim unity during the freedom struggle but in the above passage, we find that there is an everwidening gap between the Hindus and the Muslims which results in the brutal incident of the partition.

The novel provides a deep insight into the human psyche that faces trials and tribulations during the period. The characters of the novel are concerned with the national movement for independence and the novelist gives balanced views on the discussions about the non-violence, patriotism and communalism. The epigraph of the novel suggests the views and fear of Mahatma Gandhi that people misunderstood to be his ideology. He expresses his thoughts in the epigraph of the novel:

> "This non-violence, therefore, seems to be due mainly to our helplessness. It appears as if we are nursing in our bosoms the desire to take revenge the first time, we get the opportunity. Can true, voluntary non-violence come out of this seeming forced non-violence of the weak? Is it not a futile

> experiment I am conducting? What if, when the fury bursts, not a man, woman, or child is safe and every man's hand is raised against his neighbour?" (Epigraph)

The above passage shows the deep desire of Gandhi to reveal the real power of non-violence to the masses. His thoughts reflect that he was fully aware of the consequences of violence. In the novel *A Bend in the Ganges* there is a description of the violence which Gandhiji predicts in the epigraph. The novel depicts the great human drama of uprooting countless homes and the exodus of millions of people from one country to another during the partition. The novel deals with the murderous fanaticism and the inhuman slaughter on the eve of the partition. There is large scale massacre of the Hindus and the Sikhs in Lahore. The author shows how religion changes a man into a beast, "the screams of the victims rent the morning air. Someone threw a small child high in the air, and before it fell down, a man with a sword ran forward and caught it on the point of his sword". (311) In the novel the action ranges from domestic bloodshed to national tragedy. Like many other writers of the partition novel, Malgaonkar has also described some of the bloodiest scenes of the partition tragedy:

> "The large patches of red which had resembled saris left out to dry, shrank and shrivelled and faded before their eyes, leaving only pools of dried blood. The vultures, the dogs and the jackals emerged strutting disdainfully. They had pulled and torn the flesh of the bodies of the men and women striven over the field to such an extent that there was now no way of telling how much

mutilation had been inflicted by these who had attacked them." (304)

The bliss of Gandhian ideals is swept away in the anarchy and insecurity let loose by indiscriminate violence following Jinnah's call of direct action. The predominant features of the novel are its stark realism, its absolute fidelity to the truth and, above all, its trenchant exposure of the partition horrors. The theme of the book is as to how this violence affected the lives of ordinary people-men and women at that time. Malgaonkar himself admits in the author's note that,

> "Only the violence in this story happens to be true; it came to be in the wake of freedom, to become a part of India's history. what was achieved through non-violence, brought with it one of the bloodiest upheavals of history: twelve million people had to flee, leaving their homes; nearly half a million were killed; over a hundred thousand women, young and old, were abducted, raped, mutilated."

The author puts up the misapprehension of the people living on the borders that they are beyond all the looting and killing that is happening during the partition. They are in the confusion that the violence which is prevailing around them will not harm them. With the focus on one family, the author has shown this fact through the misconception of Tekchand who is not ready to leave his home town when the riots between the Hindus and the Muslims have begun. He is confined to his palace waiting for the British convoy to take him across the border to the Hindu territory. But when he wants to leave, he is totally helpless waiting for the convoy that never seems to start. He bitterly reflects: 'It was as simple as that, just two weeks ago. Get into a car and drive away' (283).

All telephone lines are cut. The suspense is sinister and scary. The novelist has thrown light on the violence of that period through Dayal and his entire family which is totally wiped out. Debi Dayal becomes the victim of the mob frenzy of the Muslims when he tries to reach his family with his beloved, Mumtaz. In the final setting we find only Debi Dayal's sister, Sundari, survives and the author leaves a faint ray of hope that she will cross the border safely with Gian, who turns up in Duriabad at a most critical moment. As a historical writer, Malgonkar draws upon his personal knowledge to create an effective backdrop for the novel. The author creates an excellent background of this scenario in his novel. He creates a vivid picture of that time and brings out the stark reality of that time. He exposes the fact that freedom came with sacrifices, violence, bloodshed, mayhem and anarchy. *A Bend in the Ganges* is "Malgaonkar's successful attempt at presenting the historical theme in fictional terms. He reveals a sound historical sense. History does not kill the spirit of the novel." (*Indian English*, Naiker, 141) Violence ruled the roost and three hundred thousand people were slaughtered as well as a hundred thousand women were raped and abducted. Some were even mutilated. Twelve million people became homeless.

The impact of Gandhian ideology is illustrated through the novel. Gandhian ideology has influenced the political as well as the social condition of India during the freedom struggle. The novelist tries to approach the Gandhian philosophy of non-violence in the light of the tragedy of the partition. The author does not endeavour to revere the image of Gandhi. The central idea of the book is to show how these two ideologies of violence and non-violence affected the common people. The two main characters of the novel represent the two different ideologies but neither of the two characters is attached to the same ideology. In the beginning of the novel, we find that Gian is following Gandhi's footsteps and Debi is prone to violence. With the help of Gian's character, the author seems to uncover the pseudo-Gandhian who only admits to follow the path of truth and non-violence but fails to understand the true meaning of Gandhian principles. The character of Gian shows weakness. He is shown burning his only foreign coat. Gian tries to defend the Gandhian way of excitement and shows his belief in Gandhi:

> "Only the Mahatma can lead us to freedom, through the path of non-violence, the creed of ahimsa... Ahimsa is the noblest of creeds. There can be nothing more sacred. No man has the right to raise his hand against another, whatever the provocation. I shall never do it. It takes greater courage; non-violence is not for the weak." (12)

The author portrays the character of Gian in such a way that suggests that Gandhian principles are not for ordinary men. The character of Gian represents the majority of the Indians who do not understand the true meaning of non-violence. He only professes to follow the path of ahimsa and calls himself a coward for not being able to save his brother. The irony of the story is that Gian, despite being non-violent, murders Vishnu Dutt to take revenge of his brother's murder. He discards the Gandhian principle of truth and non-violence. But Dinesh Chandra opines:

> "It was not the case of simple hatred and revenge that the relation demanded. It was the sacrifice of his brother for him and his career and also for his life. Hari, did not allow Gian to join his fighting with Vishnudatt and was killed before the eyes of Gian. It puts a big interrogation mark before the character of Gian who believes in the principle of non-violence. And, perhaps, this was the cause why Gian took a lot of labour to search the same axe by which Hari was killed to kill the culprit."
> (*Indian English,* Dinesh, 142)

The changes in the characters are keenly observed by the author. He brilliantly reflects the sentiments of the characters. The novelist exposes the lack of conviction and the physical cowardice in the character of Gian. Malgaonkar also shows Gian's courage for after killing Vishnudutt, he surrenders himself to the police and says, "I have just killed Vishnudatt, killed him with the same axe with which he had murdered my brother. I had to find the axe. You see, it was important that he should be killed with the same axe." (52) Gian announces himself a follower of Gandhi but the first test of his conviction finds him feeble. He realizes the fact that the Gandhian principles are not easy to follow and cannot serve as a philosophy of life. The hopes, fears and emotions of every character have been highlighted with exactness. As Ambuj Sharma comments, "The conversion of Gian Talwar from a non-violent and disciplined soldier to a reckless fellow and a killer shows the novelist's bent of mind—his sympathises with the followers of violence. The novelist, perhaps, believes that violence is inevitable in the life of every human being…" (*Gandhian Strain*, Sharma, 117)

The author focuses on how Gandhian principles have failed because of their followers. He tries to search the factors for the collapse of the Gandhian principles. The aim of the author is demeaning the Gandhian principles of truth and non-violence through the character of Gian, the confused protagonist who betrays himself and his self-professed ideals at every step of his life. Here, the comment of Bhatnagar is remarkable:

> "Whereas *ahimsain Ganges* comes off as complicated, abstract, idealistic, impracticable and only partly valid in its usually practised half – baked form, *himsa* appears more real, more natural. This presentation of *himsa* is as much material in the consideration of the treatment of Gandhian political ideology in Malgaonkar as is the sceptic note in the presentation of *ahinsa*. Debi Dayal, the positive protagonist in the novel, hold the view that *himsa* would have been a 'cleaner' alternative to *ahimsa* for fighting a war for freedom." (*Modern Indian English,* Bhatnagar, 132)

On the other hand, the characters like Debi Dayal, Shafi, Basu believe in the ideology of violence. They reflect the revolutionary activities and patriotic feelings of the young generation. Debi is fired with patriotic sentiments and forms a group of terrorists. He rejects the Gandhian ways and desires to fetch freedom through warfare and armed struggle. He deliberately chooses the way of violence and trains himself in the art of fighting. The novel gives a description of the violence and heroism of revolutionaries. The characters of Debi Dayal, Basu, Shafi Usman and other terrorists throw light on those youth who do not accept the way of non-violence or Ahimsa. Shafi who is known as Singh feels that, "College boys fall more easily for Gandhi's type of movement, it is much more face saving. They shelter their cowardice behind the tenets of non-violence, and refuse to rouse themselves to form of positive action." (12) The novel revives the picture of the terrorists' activities when the terrorist group of Debi Dayal go on cutting telephone wires, tarring the statues of the British, setting fire to the post offices, removing fish-plates and blowing up an aeroplane. The historical novelist has tried to portray a picture of the freedom struggle along with the partition in the novel and his concentration is on the political theme. The comment of Roy is noticeable:

> "Indeed, Malgaonkar is perhaps the only novelist to give importance to the terrorist movement of the 1930s; and while he concedes that Gandhi won freedom for India, there is a thorough questioning in *A Bend in the Ganges* of the validity of 'ahimsa' or non-violence. This deviation in his depiction of the diverse strands in the nationalist struggle in Malgaonkar's unique contribution to the genre of Partition fiction." (*South Asian,* Roy, 49)

It seems that the novelist tries to express his own thoughts through his characters. Tekchand who is not very interested in the political discussions of the country says that he "had never imagined that such happenings could be possible, in the middle of the twentieth century, after 30 years or so of the Mahatma's non-violence…" (282) But as the novel moves we realise that the character of Debi Dayal has undergone a great change after some bitter and mixed experiences. His character shows a leaning towards non-violence as he wondered about what Gandhi had described as man's inhumanity to man which had converted him to his doctrine of non-violence. The novelist very positively specifies the sudden changes in the thought process of both the significant characters of the novel. Both the characters gradually change their opinion and belief towards life till the end of the novel. Manohar Malgaonkar effectively demonstrates the good and bad impressions of both the ideologies through his characters in a fictitious manner. While describing the effect of the ideologies, the author is careful of not showing his leanings to either of the two ideologies.

The personal story of the main characters, their love-affairs and political alliances present the two different ideologies and philosophy of life. Both the characters have left their ideologies and are ready to embrace a life of love and peace. They are contrary to each other but they understand the value of love. After presenting all the violence and bloodbath, the novelist throws light on the importance of love through both the characters. Debi is arrested due to the betrayal of his leader terrorist, Shafi Usman. In the course of time, Debi and Gian meet in the Andaman as both have been sentenced to life imprisonment. But after their release, they find that the picture has totally changed in India. Debi, the hero wants to settle his dispute with Shafi Usman by buying his mistress, Mumtaz and wants to marry her. On the other hand, Gian loves Sundari, Debi's sister. The novelist narrates the love story of Gian-Sundari and Debi-Mumtaz in the light of tragedy of the partition. The political partition of India disturbs the Indian psyche and its social fabric. It is induction of religion into politics that has sown the seeds of the partition. However, Malgaonkar has succeeded in attempting the theme of the partition by highlighting the clash between Gandhian philosophy and the terrorist movement through a contrast between Gian's weakness and Debi's strength. But the turning point of the novel is quite different when Gian a cowardly man is ready to sacrifice everything for his love Sundari, in the same way, Debi Dayal, a brave man sacrifices his life for his love Mumtaz. Debi's love for Mumtaz is a positive force. It cuts across caste and religious barriers. The character of Debi has varying shades. He is a pathetic would-be lover in a detached manner which is simultaneously sour and soothing. Dr. A.N. Dwivedi discourses:

> "The novel shows that the urge for violence is too over-powering in man to be resisted by anything less tangible than love. It is love that transforms Debi Dayal, a terrorist into a human heart that finally seeks fulfilment in his marriage with Mumtaz. It is love that helps Gian find his true identity, the real self, filled with courage to risk even his life to protect others." (*Studies in Contemporary,* Dwivedi, 291)

The novelist wishes to emphasize on the strength of love which he does by bringing in a metamorphosis in his central characters. Malgaonkar shows the strength of love through different angles with the help of the character of Tekchand who has to leave behind his dead wife to join the convoy. He can take no more and as a compulsion vanishes when the convoy stops, probably to go back to Lahore, to go back to his mansion to be with his dead wife with all consequences therein. The depth of his love can be seen when he cannot leave his wife's dead body alone. He remembers his promise to his wife when she was dying, "No, I shall never leave you". (322) The convoy moves ahead without Tekchand, with only Sundari and Gian towards the Hindu state. The novelist wants to ensure that when all is lost, an awareness of that loss remains.

The three central characters are brilliantly depicted. There is Gian a follower of Gandhi, Debi Dayal who is an ardent terrorist and his sister Sundari who dominates the scene. The character of Sundari is depicted as a ruthless woman who holds nothing sacred and is half in love with her brother. She represents the aristocratic class of India as she is busy socialising-, playing cards, swimming and moving with Prince Amjid in clubs. Sundari is married to Gopal and makes pointless attempts to respond passionately to Gopal's love, but in vain. Gopal's indulgence in perfidy at a crucial moment in her life, puts off the spark of faith in her and her individuality rebels against tradition. She discovers her husband's relations and bonding with Malini, his friend. She talks with her faithless husband in an informal way. Gopal Chandidar represents the colonised mind of India. But his wife appears to be isolated from the political instability of the country. Sundari makes sure that she avenges herself by treating a pathetic husband by sleeping with her lover. Though the revenge is very well planned and carried out even more dramatically, she proves to her husband that she can very well pay him back in his own coin. The act of Sundari does not affect Gopal as much as it does Gian. The idealistic Gian falls in love with Sundari. She is cool and collected but concerned though distanced from Gian who seems to be an opportunist unlike her brother Debi who is a hardliner and heroic. She shakes Gian's self-confidence for his betrayal hurts her even more. But for Gian this shock is something more than he expected, for he believes that Sundari loves him. Sundari finally leaves Gopal and when Gian comes to rescue her family in Duriabad, she once again picks up on his degradation as a human being, who built his fortune on a set of immoral lies. The character of Gian reflects some changes and Sundari slowly realises those changes and accepts him though reluctantly at first. But later, she makes a man out of a liar and a cheat and establishes her genuine success as a woman. The character of Sundari depicts the quality of an Indian woman who is too progressive and revolutionary but her attitude is pure and uninhibited. Sundari, from her childhood teaches Debi to be brave and strong. She confronts Shafi and his henchmen with valour. Shafi pulls the trigger on Teckchand's wife as Sundari is too alluring. Sundari unknowingly believes in non-violence but when Shafi tries to take her with him, she kills him. Not only Sundari but also Gian takes the law into his hand and smashes the heads of all three in a frenzy of things. Malgaonkar displays the struggle of a woman with the help of the character of Sundari who tries to search her own identity as an individual. In this context M.B. Chaturvedi comments:

> "With the changing situation Manohar Malgaonkar also shows his female characters changing, curiously engaged in self-analysis, revolting against patriarchal authority, and emerging miraculously out of prolonged subjugation and abysmal darkness of their mistaken identity. They defiantly threw off their traditional legacy of humiliation, subordination and resignation, and rebelled at the idea of being

possessed or treated as a decorative article for man's pleasure." (*Indian English,* Basavaraj, 120-121)

Malgonkarunfolds this fact fully in his novel that in a changing world the moral code need not be different for man and woman. She has a right to happiness as a human being whether it is an aristocratic lady like Sundari or a prostitute like Mumtaz. She need not be tradition bound when her own mental welfare is at stake. Women of Malgonkar's novel can seek fairness and do their utmost for contentment. The analysis of women characters in the novel like Sundari and even her mother reveal the fact that like every other Indian woman they also want to depend upon men who flare up the very spark of life, adventure, and passion in their hearts and lead them step by step to fulfilment, which is the ultimate accolade to their feminineness.

The novel touches the theme of the Partition at both levels- at the community level and the individual level. The last part of the novel shows the disastrous effect of the partition at community level through riots and violence which has prevailed during the partition. The novel gives a throbbing eyewitness account of the partition episodes. At individual level, the partition affects mainly Mumtaz, Debi Dayal and his family. Debi-Mumtaz are on the way to Lahore and Debi masquerades as a Muslim. During the journey Debi and Mumtaz are surrounded by fanatic Muslims who discover Debi's identity and kill him mercilessly while they take away his beloved wife. This sudden end to Debi's life which fills the reader with remorse as tragedy strikes the upright and principled protagonist. The novel also concentrates on the psychological effect of the partition. It causes the emotional parting of people from their ancestor's land and their friends. Malgaonkar presents this pain and suffering of refugees through Tekchand who is not willing to leave his forefather's land. It is agonizing for him to abandon the place to which he belongs. He is realizing his mistake in mislaying his trust in the people of the town and does not paying heed to his wife's advice. He regrets:

> "They are my brothers, I told her. Why did I not listen to her? Because I wanted to keep all this, all that my family and I myself have built. One of the best houses in town, a name honoured in the whole province, the best private collection of Indian bronzes in the whole country. And suddenly someone has decided that this land which is mine should be foreign territory—just like that! And merely because some hooligans take it into their heads to drive all the Hindus away from their land, I have to leave everything and go, pulled out by the roots, abandoning everything that has become a part of me." (287)

The feelings and sentiments of Tekchand can be compared with Lala Kanshi Ram in Azadi who is forced to leave everything in Sialkot. The novelist gives vivid appearance of the misery of a sensitive man. Tekchand, a business man realizes that one could not get everything through money except relations and emotions. Even he is not willing to leave his dead wife and return to his home in Duriabad. This anti-climax sets this novel apart from a run of the mill plot as the writer tells a true story from the pages of history than fiction.

The partition is presented as an expression of accumulative violence. The book is the record of heart-breaking experience and dilemma of the displaced that is caused by the partition. The novelist very powerfully shows the condition of the poor people who have fallen victim to the whims of the politicians. The politicians sit impassively in their comfort zone while the minority are brutally killed by the majority. The author portrays the picture of emotional separation of people. He also highlights the fact that the pain and suffering of the common man are not noticed by the opportunist politicians. N. Sharda Iyer remarks:

> "Malgaonkar has been accused of betraying a subtle Hindu bias in the depiction of the Partition, its tragedy and riots..…But all that Malgaonkar has done is looking at it from the historical perspective and presenting a truth even if it was truth of a section of people. Moreover, Malgaonkar explores the violent reality of violence but at the same time shows how it is destructive and self-consuming." (*Musing on,* Iyer, 30)

The author very powerfully presents the feeling and sentiments of the refugees through Tekchand.

Malgonkar's style is marked by vigour and clarity. He is a master craftsman. The theme of the novel moves from personal revenge to national politics and ends with the bloodshed of the partition. The novel contains some symbolic incidents that spell out the author's awareness. The ethics in the novel are presented through symbols. The two central characters of the novel- Gian and Debi Dayal are presented as the two different ideologies of violence and non-violence. With the help of these two characters one gets an idea of the novelist's awareness. The character of Gopal symbolises the high-class aristocratic men who spend most of their time in womanising and drinking. The internal emptiness of the Hindus of Duriabad is represented by Tekchand. The terrorist activity of that time is represented by Debi, Shafi and their Hanuman club. The conflict between Shafi and Debi reflects the tension between the Hindus and Muslims. The author gives brief information about the life of prostitutes through Mumtaz.

The history of the Indian freedom struggle is depicted in a powerful way. He covers a wider canvas and presents the novel as having a radical effect on the history of the present-day. The novel encapsulates the experiences of the novelist. On 16 June 2010 Manohar Malgonkar breathed his last at Jagalpet in Karnataka's Uttara Kannada district. He was 97. As a powerful Indian English writer his works have the element of sensitivity together with a gripping and powerful story line. With his passing away the last remaining links with the Raj are slowly wearing away. Lt Col Manohar is compared with his contemporaries such as Khushwant Singh, and Mulk Raj Anand. He wrote on the conflict between the imperial power and Indians and carved a niche for himself in the realm of Indian English literature.

Works Cited

Bachchan, Ashok Kumar. "A Bend in the Ganges: A Historical Novel" *Indian English literature Vol. 6* Ed. Basavaraj Naikar New Delhi: Atlantic publishers & Distributers, 2007.

Booker, M. Keith (Ed). "The Mutiny and the Bounty: Colonial Violence and the British Power in India", *Colonial Power, Colonial Texts: India in the Modern British Novel.* USA: University of Michigan Press, 1997.

Bhatnagar, Manmohan Krishna (Ed). "The Ossifying of the Gandhian Panacea" *Modern Indian English Novel: A Critical Study of the Political Motif,* New Delhi: Atlantic Publishers and Distributors, 2003.

Chaturvedi, M.B. "Feminist Consciousness in the Novels of Manohar Malgaonkar" *Indian English literature Vol. 6* Ed. Basavaraj Naikar New Delhi: Atlantic publishers & Distributers, 2007.

Dwivedi A.N., "The Historian as Novelist: Manohar Malgaonkar" *Perspectives on Indian Fiction in English* Ed. M.K. Naik, New Delhi: Abhinav Publication, 1985.

Dwivedi, A.N. (Ed) "Manohar Malgaonkar: The novelist and his Point of View", *Studies in Contemporary Indian Fiction in English,* Allahabad: Kitab Mahal, 1987.

Iyer, N. Sharda (Ed) "Manohar Malgaonkar's Tryst with Destiny: A Bend in the Ganges" *Musing on Indian Writing in English: Fiction* New Delhi: Sarup & Sons, 2003.

Kumar, Dinesh Chandra. "A Bend in the Ganges: Ideology and Conviction" *Indian English Literature: A Post-*

Colonial Response Ed. Gajendra Kumar & Uday Shankar Ojha. New Delhi: Sarup & Sons, 2005.

Malgaonkar, Manohar. *A Bend in the Ganges,* New Delhi: Saurabh Printers, 1964. (All the subsequent references given in the parenthesis are from this edition)

Roy, Rituparna (Ed). South Asian Partition Fiction in English: From Khuswant Singh to Amitav Ghosh, Amsterdam: Amsterdam University Press, 2010.

Sharma, Ambuj Kumar (Ed). "Gandhi and the Emergent India: Shadow from Ladhak and A Bend in the Ganges", *Gandhian Strain in the Indian English Novel,* New Delhi: Sarup & Sons, 2004.

AZADI

Azadi is a mammoth novel which exposes the cruel and disastrous story of the division of the Indian sub-continent into India and Pakistan. The theme is alluring because it is concerned with the history as well as literature of our country. It receives the attention of many novelists and one of them is Chaman Nahal. He has brilliantly fictionalized the acrimonious event of the partition as the major theme in his novel *Azadi*. It is one of the optimum realistic novels on the theme of partition. The novel added a new feather to Chaman Nahal's cap, when it received the Sahitya Akadami Award. Basavaraj comments:

> "Chaman Nahal (1927) is hailed as a brilliant Indian English novelist of the second generation. He has enriched the field of political fiction which is very poor as compared to other forms of Indian English Fiction *Azadi* offers an intensive picture of the effect of the traumatic experience of the partition of the country into India and Pakistan on the life of the people living in the north-western border area of India." (*Modern Indian,* Chandra, 129)

It seems that Nahal has put his soul into the writing of this book because it is based on the real and bitter experiences of the novelist. The novel highlights one of the most fateful and traumatic events of Indian history, the partition. It narrates the trauma and havoc of post-independent India at the time of the partition of India. The author was greatly moved by the harrowing events during those turbulent days. The novel also throws light on Chaman Nahal's views on politics. He regards the political process with disdain. Nahal accentuates the fact that the Indians were fighting for one country, India, but later the battle for freedom changed into the two-nation theory. The impact of the partition has been realistically expressed with scornful irony in the novel. It is a story about the lives and aspirations of the Hindu and Muslim immigrants during the partition. The book is replete with scenes of terror and violence as millions of Hindus, Sikhs and Muslims flee to the new territories of Pakistan and India. It reflects the fateful story of political hatred and violence during the partition of British India when the spirit of communal frenzy was fuming within the masses. The objective of the novelist is to highlight the socio-economic theme and lands of their birth. K.S. Ramamurti rightly remarks, "The author of *Azadi* presents, therefore, a great historical event in terms of its full human implications seen and felt through the lives of a few individuals." (*Three Contemporary,* Dhawan, 132)

The novel has a well-taut structure. It is unique and different in its realistic presentation. It has an enthralling narrative with comprehensible and recognizable characters. The idea of structure includes area of plot, the sequence of events, the narrative and episodic arrangements. The novelist has shown vitality and variety in his writing. *Azadi* is the result of Chaman Nahal's artistic craftsmanship and creative genius. The novel reflects humanity and artistic honesty of the novelist. The main element of the plot is the profound sensitive transformation and the unfathomable mental instabilities which are brought by the tormenting experiences of the partition. The novel is divided into three parts: (I) "The Lull", (II) "The Storm", (III) "The Aftermath". The subtitles themselves suggest what these parts contain. The titles of the three parts of the novel present the multi-coloured and multi-faceted picture of a turbulent phase of Indian history. The three sections of the novel represent the beginning, the middle and the end of the description of the psychological and emotional effect of the partition on the personal and general planes.

The title "Azadi" symbolises the freedom which India achieved in 1947 after a long heroic struggle from the tyrannical rule of the British, but the theme of the novel is treated ironically because the joy of the freedom is overshadowed by the tragedy of the partition of the sub-continent which led to domestic war and generated anguish, embarrassment and blood-bath in every corner of the country. On the eve of the partition of the Indian subcontinent, millions of people from both sides of the dividing boundary were on the way, looking for shelter and safety. Many of the Hindus and the Sikhs left their home and land in Pakistan and forced a passage to India. In the same way, millions of Muslims from India left their memories with their ancestral place and sought their way to Pakistan. Thus, communities were torn from their roots and 'azadi' which India had attained from the British rule was the cause of the harrowing process of this change. Azadi i.e. our freedom is the witness of the awful and ghastly experience of human beings involved in a historical, impersonal and brutalised process.

The novel, *Azadi,* is like an epic which presents the different aspects of life with "its predominant colours—the red and the black—and the dizzy whirr of events are but foils to the white flame of the eternal human values of love and sympathy steadily burning through the novel and the necessity and fruitfulness of individual action which it ends." (*Studies in Contemporary*, Dwievdi, 323)

Like Attia Hosain, Nahal confronted all the adversities during the partition. He was born, and grew up in Sialkot and was forced to leave after the partition. He "can understand the suffering and loneliness that such an exile imposes on the persons involved in a class by itself." (*Three Contemporary,* Dhawan, 96)

Perhaps, this is the reason that he has taken the darkest part of Indian history as the theme of his novel which is treated by many historians as well as novelists. Being a historical novelist, Nahal focuses on the history of the partition and the human suffering, violence and pathetic condition of refugees. The novelist is deeply hurt by the brutal incident of the partition. He describes a kind of grisly, macabre atmosphere that has its own sharp appeal. The novel is really a masterpiece because it presents the spacious vision and optimistic view of the author. It has shown the influence of the Hindu religion with the element of Indian sensibility. It represents Indian life and philosophy. Nahal is so fixated with the essence of Indianness that he has given a Hindi title to his English novel. The protagonist Lala Kanshi Ram represents a typical Indian character. Lala Kanshi Ram is a major figure on the dramatic stage of *Azadi*. Despite all the hurdles, suffering, pains and trauma of the partition, Lala Kanshi Ram begins his life from scratch. The realism in the novel is reflected at various levels with the basic conflict due to opposing forces. The novel succeeds in its aim of depicting the agony of a whole great country and at the same time telling us something about human nature in all its richness. The setting of the novel is laid on the eve of the partition in 1947 in Sialkot, Pakistan. The Hindus, Sikhs and Muslims form the community of Sialkot city who have lived together peacefully for centuries. The novelist keeps his finger on the pulse of Sialkot while portraying the changing patterns of communal relations between the Hindus and the Muslims. Division and disharmony are the ruling principles of the world of Sialkot during the partition. The fiction writer has described the atrocities perpetuated by the two communities upon each other. The social and religious beliefs and divisions of Sialkot community are highlighted against a larger world which is also divided. Forces of division alternate with religious forces of union. The novel shows the strength of communal harmony during the pre-Partition period, when in Dusschra festival, " huge effigies of Ravana and his evil associates were burned to the ground, every year. It was a Hindu festival but the effigies were made by Muslim workmen; the crackers and the fireworks too were supplied by the Muslims." (*Azadi*, Nahal, 75)

But during communal slaughter of Partition, "…there was one thing common to them all: the brutality of the act. In no case was the victim allowed to survive the attack and tell what happened; he was stabbed to death…Where the victim survived the first blow, he was repeatedly stabbed in the chest and the abdomen." (105)

The Hindus and the Muslims are shown in bitter enmity during the migration of people across the Radcliff line. But at the same time, the intensity of communal harmony between the two communities of the same place is never shown to have been corrupted. How the emotions of the people are aroused by the rumours spread by each community about the barbaric deeds of the other, is described by Chaman Nahal through the mounting tension between the Hindus and the Muslims who had lived in perfect amity for many years before the recent trouble in Sialkot, "Unless you had another Muslim to vouch for you, you were rudely undressed by the mob and your vitals exposed to the curious eyes. 'Kill him—he is a Kafir!' and the knife was driven at once through your stomach." (149) The novel tells the story of inhuman behaviour that is adopted by the Muslims because they want to eradicate the Hindus.

A background of terror and the panic among the Hindus and the Sikhs of Sialkot is effectively created. The tone of this novel is set right from the first line through a proficient depiction of horror, gruesome and perilous surroundings in which the feeling of affection and love seemed to be drying up. With its wide canvas, the novel covers a period of seven months. The purpose of taking the period of only seven months is to show that although the time of seven months is very minor but the consequences were radical and long-lasting in the Indian history. The novel ends with the catastrophic death of Gandhiji on January 30th 1948. Nahal deliberately chooses the ending of his novel with the dark clouds cast by the great Mahatma's death to show how the biggest follower of non-violence is killed by violence, "It was no ordinary light, he said, it was a most extraordinary flame. It was gone and India was plunged into darkness." (320)

Chaman Nahal, like Manohar Malgaonkar emphasizes the fact that at that time, the element of non-violence had failed because of the kind of followers they had. They did not understand the hidden meaning of non-violence. In the fictionalization of Gandhi's assassination, the novelist points out the undignified influence of the evil of narrow-mindedness and violence on the young minds. The murder of Gandhiji signifies the end of the traumatic event which starts seven months before and the entire upheaval comes to an end with his death. Nahal was greatly influenced by Gandhi's personality. Thus, he writes:

> "Here was a man who in ten years' time had revolutionized the spirit of the country. There was not a city in India where Gandhi's name was not known. And he talked of peace in place of war and he talked of non-violence in place of violence, and yet he also talked of fighting with the British on his own special terms." (84)

The effect of Gandhi's teaching and non-violence is clearly shown through the novel. Lala Kanshi Ram, like Mahatma Gandhi, tries to maintain peace through non-violence when the young boys of Sikhs and Hindus want to teach a lesson to the Muslims. Lala Kanshi Ram was strongly rooted in Indian tradition. He is the representative of a typical Indian of his time. He embodies the spirit of Gandhiji and suffers a lot like him. He has great respect for Gandhi and is shaken by Gandhi's death. As Rama Jha says, "He is deliberately modelled in a Gandhian character to register Gandhi's death as a personal loss." (Review, Jha)The tormenting and traumatic events connected with the partition are presented mainly through the family of Lala Kanshi Ram, a grain merchant in the city of Sialkot. He represents the regrets and miseries of the affected millions of the Hindus, the Sikhs and the Muslims equally. The novel starts in the bazaar lanes of Sialkot, with a vibrant community of Muslims and Hindu families. The environment that is created reflects the uncomfortable calm that prevails before the storm of the partition of the country. Through the character of Lala Kanshi Ram, the novelist also highlights various political issues influencing the fate of the country and its people. Right from the first line, the novelist skilfully uses the atmosphere of anxiety and worry in creating the genuine picture of the city of Sialkot "It was the third of June, 1947. This evening, the Viceroy was to make an important announcement." (1) Beginning with a description like this, an atmosphere of gloom is created and the events that are about to occur seem unavoidable. The novel represents an unexpected tension that carries throughout the day in Sialkot. The date is important because the Viceroy has announced the partition and from that day Pakistan has come into existence officially. After that, the major community starts torturing the minor community and the forces of wickedness are let loose on both sides of border. The delight and enjoyment of the partition in the novel has been attached to the Muslim community where as the fear, frustration, the desperation and the sense of loss to the Hindus of Sialkot. The Muslims of Sialkot take out a procession through the market— dancing and shouting, "Pakistan Zindabad! Long Live Pakistan!" (56) They are trying to make a forced entry into the Hindu area while on the other side the frightened and anxious Hindu families watch the procession from their roofs.

The narrative brings to light the enormity of political decisions at the time of independence and partition in the form of Lala Kanshi Ram's apprehensions about the situation:

> "He had his fears since February, when the British set up a time limit for independence. They had clearly committed themselves; they had said that not later than June 1948, India would have its azadi. They also said if the Indian political parties did not agree on a solution by then, the British would hand power over to any constituted authority or authorities of the moment; but they must quit. It was this that disturbed Lala Kanshi Ram. Good, India would be free. But why were they in a hurry to leave? And why this reference to freedom in plural? Didn't that mean they were thinking of Pakistan?" (27)

The description of Lala Kanshi Ram's actions and attitudes are notable. The reaction of Lala Kanshi Ram helps the reader to understand the enormity of the incident. The novelist has tried to search the real source and origin of the tragic event. Here, Nahal presents the mistrust and bewilderment of the minorities through Kanshi Ram who believes that Mahatma Gandhi shall never agree for the partition. According to Lala Kanshi Ram, the partition of the sub-continent is not coherent in any way. The Congress policy has come under detailed criticism in the novel:

> "The Congress had a promise to keep with the people. For the last thirty years, since that wizard Gandhi came on the scene, it had taken the stand that India was a single nation, not two. And

THE THEME OF THE PARTITION

> Gandhi was not only a politician, he was a saint. He had his inner voice to satisfy too. Would that nagging voice of his let him accepts the slaughter of so many? That's what it would mean, if Pakistan did come into existence. And Gandhi was shrewd—surely, he saw it all. He wouldn't give in to such butchery. If nothing else worked, his fasts unto death always did. (35)."

Gandhiji is the hope of millions like Kanshi Ram. People believe in Gandhi's wisdom and his power to control any situation effectively has come under great shock. In the mood of retrospection, he thinks about Gandhi's speech when he visited Sialkot. The author has introduced the tour of Gandhi in Sialkot, in order to bring up some of the foremost features of Gandhian ideology like self-sacrifice and non-violence. It also provides the author an opportunity to emphasise on the importance of the Hindu-Muslim unity as desired by Gandhi which is symbolised by the relationship of Chaudhari Barkat Ali and Lala Kanshi Ram. They wear home-made 'khaddar' because they know that wearing foreign cloth, "deprived the Indian workman of his labour and it prolonged the British rule here by that much time." (87) Gandhi has declared that India will not divide on communal basis. The Muslim community is a part of India but the British are not. The reason is that the former had settled here. He feels, "A Muslim in India was more an Indian than anything else. The same was true of a Hindu. His gods came much lower in rank than the motherland which had given him birth." (87) Gandhi's speech held Kanshi Ram spellbound. The influential speech of Gandhi makes him believe that partition will never happen, but all is in vain. Now at the time of the partition, he is so disturbed that he criticizes Gandhi for giving importance to Jinnah. The novel focuses on the causes and consequences of the partition from the perspective of the major characters like Lala Kanshi Ram, Arun and Barkat Ali. According to Kanshi Ram, it is only Gandhi and Rajaji, who have given importance to Jinnah and implanted the idea of Pakistan. His opinion and belief was expressed in following words:

> "Didn't Gandhiji and Rajaji themselves as much as offer Pakistan to Jinnah in 1944? They were the ones who put the idea in his head...take a section in the East of India and a section in the West, they said. Only let's have a common defence and foreign policy. Until then Jinnah had talked about Pakistan, but he did not quite know what he meant by it. Gandhi by going to him, not only gave Pakistan a name, he gave Jinnah a name too. Who took Jinnah seriously before September 1944?" (27)

Like millions of people, Kanshi Ram who trusts Gandhi does not understand the actual cause that forces the Mahatma to agree for the partition. Gandhi's teaching of non-violence had vanished from the masses during the partition. People only knew the language of religion and hatred at that time. Reflecting his own personal experiences, Nahal writes:

> "After 1947, he made Birla House in New Delhi his home. Our family by then had migrated from Pakistan to New Delhi, and it was possible for me to attend Gandhi's prayer meetings on most evenings. And what caught my eyes was the immense humility of the man. Many of us among his listeners were angry young men who had lost

everything in Pakistan, including the dear ones who were assassinated in the riots. And we asked Gandhi angry questions. To which he never gave an answer without making us feel that our pain was his pain too." (*Three Contemporary,* Dhawan, 39)

The novelist highlights a politics polluted society where people of both religions were mere puppets in the hands of the British rulers and short-sighted national leaders who were blind to this horrendous catastrophe. The writer has focused on the British policy of divide and rule with which they conquered India. In the novel, at first Lala Kanshi Ram represents the colonised mind that, "enjoyed the safety of the British Raj" and believes that the British has brought peace and justice to this land. He is a great fan of the British because "there had been less bloodshed in India in the two hundred years of British Raj than in any similar period in the past."(8) It is notable that the British coloniser succeeded in invading the mind of the colonised through the character of Lala Kanshi Ram who considers it to be a matter of pride to be a faithful admirer of the British. His conviction and confidence are crushed by both the national leaders and the British, "after a long time, Lala Kanshi Ram felt bitter against the English ....Yes, they were the real villians; they had let the country down—they had let him down, he who put such faith in them." (118) His expectation has been crumpled by the moves and motives of the British. S.C. Bhatta opines in his review of Azadi:

"His attitude towards the British Raj is marked with an element of ambiguity. On the one hand, he is moved by the patriotic feelings to free his country, on the other hand, he likes the pageants and processions, and safety and security of the British Raj. He fails to see the drastic dimensions of Hindu-Muslim hostility which is destined to take place in a few weeks." (*Literary Criterion*, Bhatta, 228)

Like many other novelists, Chaman Nahal has criticised the British rule. But he has respect for the discipline, decency and protection of the British rule. The novelist has commented on the part played by the educated people of the country making sarcastic comments on the freedom, azadi. He has tried to give a picture which shows that the partition is the result of the leaders' mutual failure because the process of the partition is over in a flash and they have failed to recognize the real face of the time which has brought the tumultuous event of the partition. The novelist focuses on *Azadi* as a political novel with the main stress on human values and human beings. *Azadi* brings out effectively the irony in the following words that is the basis of the novel. Arun, the son of Lala Kanshi Ram, observes the political moves and their impact on masses. Nahal clearly states:

"He knew the conspiracy of politicians behind the whole move. Jinnah and Liakat Ali Khan were coming into an estate, as was Nehru. Why else would they rush into azadi at this pace –an azadi which would ruin the land and destroy its unity? For the creation of Pakistan solved nothing. One would have to go around with tweezers through all the villages to separate the Muslims from the Hindus. Arun knew this, the game of which he and Nur and millions like them were victims. But politicians gave ideas legs, even though they were the wrong kind of ideas." (78).

In the voice of Lala Kanshi Ram, Chaman Nahal denounces the leaders of the Congress, the Muslim league and Akali Dal for the partition. Azadi focuses on the historical figures of that time. Among them he puts guilt mainly on Jinnah, Nehru, Baldev Singh, Rajaji and Kriplani who failed to understand the communal dynamics. The novelist's primary concern is not dealing with the political matters but their impact on individual lives which gets a psychological strengthening on account of their being presented against the stormy background of the tragedy of the partition. It is through the families of Lala Kanshi Ram and those around him like Sardar Niranjan Singh, Chandini, Sunanda and Bibi AmarVati that Nahal unfolds the terror of the riots and tragedy of the partition. In the opinion of Kanshi Ram, the national leaders should have planned proper means of mass migration before rushing hastily to partition the country and that is why he considers Kriplani, "the worst offender", because he did not think about the minorities and without taking any step to protect the minorities he asked them to stay where they were. Chaman Nahal affirms that the material and spiritual focus is the human being rather than merely the historical context in the novel. The remark of A.H. Tak is remarkable in this context:

> "A very distinctive novel in terms of subject matter, technique and tone but characterized by an exploration of the relationship between history and fiction, Chaman Nahal's *Azadi* -a partition novel expresses strong consciousness of the 'fictiveness'

of all discourse about reality and history."(Akademi Awarded, Tak, 110)

Nahal presents the character of Kanshi Ram as a victim of the minorities of both the religions who have suffered the pangs of the partition. These people are betrayed by their power-hungry politicians and "now they should at least keep their mouths shut and not mislead the poor, credulous people. Jinnah and Nehru were villains enough. This President of the Indian National Congress...." (183). Here, Chaman Nahal deliberately mentions the names of Jinnah and Nehru because both of them are representative of their community. As Jinnah is criticized by the Indian Muslims, in the same way, Nehru is criticized by the Hindus of Pakistan because in both the countries, the minorities are incensed at the decision of the partition. They are deliberately thrown in the gory incidents of the partition by their ambitious leaders. R.K. Dhawan rightly remarks, "Nahal has studied the partition dispassionately and his observations are just and impartial. He does not apportion the guilt; he narrates with fidelity what had happened and the manner in which it had happened." (*Three Contemporary,* Dhawan, 25)

Nahal believes that it was the Muslim League that deceived its own people and spread misleading information regarding the Hindus and Sikhs. Jinnah highlighted small problems among the parties for his own benefit and pushed the country towards the partition. The leaders of the Muslim League inflamed hatred among simple people to serve their own selfish ends. They were manipulated and involved in violence by Jinnah's call of direct action. The author throws light on the gradual changes in the society and the changes in the relations of the Hindus and the Muslims. Nahal also shows how Kanshi Ram the Hindu, Barkat Ali the Muslim, and Teja Singh the Sikh share the same Punjabi culture and language, and consider Sialkot their homeland. The Muslim league and Jinnah used the innocent people just to fulfill their hunger for power and to prove this fact Nahal paints the character of Abdul Ghani, a hookah manufacturer, who was very friendly with Kanshi Ram in pre-partition days. Now, he calls Kanshi Ram a Kafir. Lala Kanshi Ram is shocked at the sheer venom of Abdul Ghani. The changes in the nature and attitude of Abdul Ghani represent the changes in the Muslim society. He, like any other Muslim, starts hating his Hindu friends and neighbours because his leaders have told him to do so. The author observes the character of Abdul Ghani very minutely:

> "The Muslim League had slowly made him aware of the threat to him in a free Hindu India. It was not a question of his personal views; the league or Jinnah Sahib knew better. They said, view your Hindu neighbour with suspicion, and he did that. They said there should be a Pakistan, and he shouted for it." (42)

This is what we can say is the gift of the Muslim League to his Hindu friends. Like Nahal, Attia Hosain has also described the gradual changes in conservative Muslims through the character of Saleem who starts opposing Congress and supporting the two-nation theory of M.A. Jinnah after joining the Muslim League. The nature and attitude of both the characters are same. But there is one difference between them; Saleem represents the reputed and higher-class Muslims whereas Abdul Ghani shows the mental situation of poor and ordinary Muslims. But both of them are influenced by the policy of Jinnah and the Muslim League.

Nahal also holds Nehru responsible for the partition and berates him for his frail and fake promises about the partition. But he also appreciates him as a 'brilliant' and 'proud leader' who was so popular that, "his people were indulgent of him, the crowds would laugh at his temper and dismiss his angry words as the prank of a 'king'." (49) He is also unhappy with the partition and while announcing it, his sound is 'meek and gentle' and 'in sorrow'. The acclaim for Nehru shows that the author presents his views without any bias. He appreciated Nehru for his vital role in getting India free. But his speech on partition had prompted an angry response from both Hindu and Sikh's of Sialkot. Lala Kanshi Ram is confused and incoherent after the broadcast because Nehru's speech is beyond reality. He said that the leaders were ready to make sacrifices, 'we're willing to make sacrifices' (50) but Kanshi Ram did not understand the type of sacrifices leaders would make? The Hindus and Sikhs of Sialkot are in dismay when they hear about the partition because their chances of survival in Pakistan are beyond hope. They bleat about their future and survival. And the author admonishes Nehru for his meaningless speech:

> "What happened to his *akal*, his mind? Have partition if there is no other way. But what nonsense is this of no panic, no violence, full protection from the government, peace the main object! Had he gone mad? Didn't he know his people? Didn't he know the Muslims? And why the partition in the first place? What of your promises to us, you Pandit Nehru?" (50)

Here, the questions of Kanshi Ram symbolize the feelings of anger and frustration of refugees who betrayed by their leaders are indisposed to the idea of the partition. The novel presents the remarks of common people on the nature of the political situation and the role of politics in their lives forcing them to accept the unacceptable. Nahal emphasizes the point that Nehru has failed to fulfill his promise to protect the minorities in India as well as in Pakistan. The leaders of all communities ignore the fact that it is in vain to expect peace and non-violence from the major community, when so much violence and hatred is in the air. In such an inflamed situation, it is natural that people of a particular community have feelings of hatred for the other community. Jinnah only thinks about Pakistan but not about the Indian Muslims who become the victim of the partition. As Chaman Nahal is asking Nehru about his promises, in the same way, Attia Hosain asks this question to Jinnah about his false promises and duties that he has towards his community. He is more responsible for the partition. The partition of the sub-continent is extremely repulsive for all communities. The country was in a state of political turmoil at that time and it is very clearly shown by the novelist. Kanshi Ram is the spokesperson of the Hindus, in the same way; Laila is the speaker of the Muslims in *Sunlight on a Broken Column.* Both criticize their leaders for not protecting the minorities. Sardar Niranjan Singh, a young and strong Sikh is shocked to listen that his Akali Dal has also accepted the decision of the partition without thinking of the Sikhs who are in Pakistan. He is so angry with Nehru that he wants to "take out his sword and hack Nehru to pieces." (51) The author has highlighted the fact that it is an indubitable fact that the British are responsible for the tumultuous event of the partition but our leaders are more responsible for it. The fate of millions of people is decided by a few leaders.

Chaman Nahal presents a different point of view through Bill Davidson, British officer, and an intimate friend of Arun and Munir. According to him, Indian leaders should be united in their demands. They should move towards freedom carefully and slowly because "haste will lead to fragmentation." (99) He has a sympathetic and kind attitude towards India. In that concern, he opines heatedly that the way through which India is getting her freedom "is the most stupid, most damaging, most negative, development in the history of the freedom struggle here." (101) The reason of presenting the character of Bill Davidson is to expose the guilt and mistakes committed by the Indian leaders. In their rush towards getting freedom for the country, Indian leaders forget that the country consists of millions of people of many communities and not few leaders. Bill Davidson supports the Cabinet Mission plan and condemns that the Indian leaders throw many proposals but not a single one that keeps India united. This can be considered as a true and honest clarification because the person is neither a Hindu nor a Muslim. He judges the Indian leaders very closely and tells his friend Arun and Munir:

> "You may sing songs in honour of Mountbatten... But he has duped you into a division of the country. Even Gandhi and Nehru failed to hold their balance before him-Jinnah I never counted for much. They have all fallen for a handy prize, not realizing the misery it will heap on the masses." (102)

The comment of Bill Davidson reveals the fact that all the communities, the Hindus, the Sikhs, the Muslims and even the British understand the hazardous and life-threatening situation of our country except our leaders. He does not estimate Jinnah as a capable and efficient leader. He has respect for Gandhi and Nehru but even they do not understand the real interest of Mountbatten which is in the partition of the country. In the words of Lala Kanshi Ram, Nahal himself criticizes the British for their failure to protect the minorities as well as the country from the partition, "It was their job, their obligation, to see that freedom came smoothly. If today the man in the street feels insecure and if the government is powerless to protect his life and property, I hold the English responsible for that crime." (118)

There are many factual events in the novel that help the author in his thematic concerns. The novel begins in mid-1947 with the people of Sialkot hear the announcement regarding partition, but they refuse to believe that they now have to move. The original beliefs of unity in the soul of the people of Sialkot are defeated by the religious diversities. Sialkot city which was the symbol of peace and unity suddenly becomes the picture of religious disharmony and disunity. Abdul Ghani who was a good friend of Lala Kanshi Ram in pre-partition days, suddenly starts calling him a Kafir. The birth of Pakistan has made him aware of his identity as a Muslim. His bitterness comes out when he speaks with Lala Kanshi Ram:

'Why do you want me to leave Abdul Ghani?' said Lala Kanshi Ram. 'We have been good friends—for years we have been such good friends!'

Abdul Ghani was taken aback at this. He had many other nasty things he wanted to say to Lala Kanshi Ram; he couldn't bring one of them out. Deflated, he sat on the wooden platform and looked at the ground.

Remembering he was speaking to a Kafir after all, he flared up again.

'I want you to leave because you're a Hindu, and you don't believe in Allah.' (112)

The changed behaviour of Abdul Ghani hurts Lala Kanshi Ram.The character of Abdul Ghani sheds light on the thinking of the Muslims of lower class in Sialkot. Abdul Ghani, a hookah manufacturer, has hated Lala Kanshi Ram and other Hindus because they are not followers of Islam. Chaman Nahal emphasizes the fact that the Muslims like Abdul Ghani are in ignorance about the true teaching of Islam. They are totally influenced by the atmosphere which is prevailing in Sialkot. In the case of Abdul Ghani, Nahal has focused on one fact which is history, that the lower and middle class Muslims belonging to Hinduism in the past converted to Islam during the Muslim rule, "historical truth that he was the product of many crosses between the low caste Hindu women and Mogul foot soldiers" (37) But they have forgotten this truth and consider themselves a separate race and the Muslim League has used all its energy to make them believe that the Hindus are their biggest enemy on this earth. Abdul Ghani who is so bitter that on the death of Arun's sister he says, "I put her and her husband into the fire with my own hands, and they're now on their way to dozakh, to hell—where I hope they rot forever!" (159) The violence and hatred are the inseparable elements of the air in Sialkot. The feelings of love and non-violence have been wiped out from people's heart. In contrast to Abdul Ghani, we have Chaudhari Barkat Ali. Some characters act as foils to each other. Barkat Ali and Kanshi Ram are like brothers more than friends. He is filled with sadness and regret when Kanshi Ram is forced to leave Sialkot. The behaviour of Abdul Ghani infuriates Barkat Ali. He provides Kanshi Ram all possible help. He warns him about the Muslim attack that is going to happen in his street at night. He has saved his friend's life and fulfilled his responsibility as a true friend. The novelist presents his character in the following words:

> "More than anything else, he regarded himself and his family as good Muslims because they believed in the unity of all religions. There was not a single ayat, a single verse, in the Quran which preached otherwise. God is great and Muhammad is his prophet. But the same God is the God of the Hindus as well, and if they preferred to worship him in another form that was their business. It was not for Barkat Ali to go round correcting the world. His job was to live the life God had given him in friendship and love. And the Hindu next door was as much his brother, more his brother, than an unknown Muslim living elsewhere." (83-84)

Religion cannot be the cause of destruction, and discrimination on grounds of religion will not be tolerated, that is what Nahal wants to say through the character of Chaudhari Barkat Ali. He was not influenced by the communal violence. He is undoubtedly a follower of love, tolerance and friendship. Chaudhari Barkat Ali is a significant character because he presents the quality of not only a true Muslim but also a good human being. The friendship of Lala Kanshi Ram and Barkat Ali give some relief amidst the violence of the partition tragedy.

The author has shown the pathetic and miserable condition of the Hindus and Sikhs in Sialkot. He has described a bizarre situation in which the minorities of Sialkot city bear the atrocities committed by the police, the army and above all the government itself. Chaman Nahal's *Azadi* have their source in Indian's partition and the communal riots that preceded and followed it. The fact is highlighted by Nahal openly that the Pakistan government is helping the rioters and are far from being impartial. Suddenly, out of the blue, Barkat Ali informs Lala Kanshi Ram that Hindu Deputy Commissioner has been shot by his Muslim bodyguard or constable. Barkat Ali believes that the latter will not be punished but "the Pakistani government will bestow a medal on him." (117) The view of Barkat Ali reflects the light on the role of the government of Pakistan in communal violence. It is not very difficult for the government to control violence and maintain law and order in the city but if the government is seen to condone violence, the bloodshed will never stop. Even they do not provide any protection for refugees who are ready to go to India leaving their property and everything behind in Pakistan, "the liaison officer Major Jang Bahadur Singh left behind in Pasrur said the Pakistani authorities were creating obstructions on purpose. He warned the Major that the convoy might be attacked by the local Muslims…. He feared it was to help the mob that the Pakistani authorities were not letting them depart." (247-248) The author exposes the real and ugly face of the Pakistan government who is not interested for the safety of the Hindus and the Sikhs, instead of that it wants to torture and humiliate them. Rahmat-Ull-Khan and Inayat-

Ull-Khan are the government officers who whole heartedly help the rioters. Inayat-Ull-Khan, a police officer, finds a Muslim procession is not being allowed to go through a Hindu mohalla. He immediately, without thinking about the Hindus and Sikhs, orders the Sub-inspector to "break open the gate" (64) and when they do not follow his order, he orders them separately and deliberately just to "watch a Sikh order other Sikhs to their destruction." (65) In opposition of him, there is one character—Bill Davidson, who belongs to the community against which Hindus and Muslims were fighting together. But here, we see that a British helps a Hindu family against the Muslims. He presents the image of an ideal person and friend. Bill Davidson brings a truck and takes them safely to a refugee camp. Rahmat-Ull-Khan, the camp commander and an army officer is an ardent Muslim who gets an opportunity to rape Sunanda who is daughter-in-law of Kanshi Ram's landlady, Bibi Amar Vati. People of the minority community have well known the reality that these officers have "their separate communal loyalties. These loyalties were openly and unashamedly expressed." (183) The novelist stresses on the strange and disgraceful behaviour of these government officers. Instead of protecting the minorities, they are manipulating and humiliating them. The author has given the character of Hakim Sahib who is a Muslim but feels sad on the parade of naked women. The inference has been drawn from his showing that Hakim Sahib has been large hearted enough not to support any activity against the Hindus. He finds the parade of naked Hindu women in streets of Narowal as a sign of brutality by the members of his community. The narrator records the reaction of the Hakim Sahib in the following words:

"The hakim sahib had covered his face with his hands and was rocking a little and he was saying, 'Allah, Allah, Allah!' And then he knelt on his knees, raised his arms and spread his hands before him while saying namaaz. There was the look of infinite pain on his face. His thin, frail eyelids rested on his eyes as if they would never open again. And moving his outstretched hands, like begging alms, he murmured in Punjabi, 'Rabbul-Alamin, forgive these cruel men. And, oh, my Allah, oh Rabbah, protect these women." (262-263)

Being a Muslim, he is praying for Hindu women which clearly shows that he is neither a non-believer nor a non-Muslim. The reaction of Hakim Sahib signifies that he has not been overpowered by communal passion. He has closed his eyes that shows that he has seen the most hateful and disgusting scene of his life. Now he does not want to see anything else. The character of Hakim Sahib is different because as a Muslim, he is praying to God to forgive the cruel and guilty members of his community for their evil deeds which shows that he is really worried about his Muslim brothers. And on other hand, he is also praying for Hindu women that displays his humanity and sympathy towards the vulnerable women. Arun wants to hate the whole community of the Muslims for such evil and cruel activities but he is shocked and confused to see Hakim Sahib. Later on, while in Amritsar, he comes to know about a similar parading of naked Muslim women. Though he does not see it but he hears the lewd comments and abuses hurled at those hapless women. Seeing the dome of Golden Temple in the background, he wonders if any Sikh out there is weeping for these women. The passage reveals the author's view that although the Muslims of Sialkot have tortured the Hindus and the Sikhs but some people from the same community do not support the evil and wicked deeds of the cruel members of the community. In *Train to Pakistan* Khushwant Singh has also shown the same humanity through his character Juggut Singh who sacrifices his life in order to save the lives of the Muslims leaving on the train going to Pakistan. Here, we can find that the author seems to exhort the reader to see the positive aspect of every character and situation.

The entire Muslim community is not involved in violence. Nahal has painted both types of characters—good and bad to prove that religion is not responsible for these evil deeds. If Nahal has painted the bad and evil characters like Abdul Ghani, Rahmat-Ull-Khan and Inayat-Ull-Khan to show how religion is responsible to change a man into a beast, he also portrays the characters of Bill Davidson, Barkat Ali and Hakeem Sahib as a symbol of humanity, kindness, love and sympathy to prove that humanity can arouse the most exalting, inspiring and beautiful desire in man. The purpose of the narrator to paint these characters is to bring out the fact that some members of the Muslim community and the British stand for communal harmony. They make efforts to make it succeed. Bill Davidson and Barkat Ali are the two important persons who support Lala Kanshi Ram at his crucial time. One is a British and the other is a Muslim. Lala Kanshi Ram blames the British as the major reason of the partition and curses the Muslims for the violence which they have started after the announcement of the partition. But these two characters from the novel have cleared the fact that no one can blame the whole community for any incident. Attia Hosain also highlights this fact through her characters like Sita and Ranjeet who have saved the life of Laila during communal violence in India.

The novelist gives a realistic account of the riots which started in 1947 as a result of the partition of the sub-continent. The riots in the first part are the symbol of violence. The novel deals with the theme of the partition followed by communal bloodshed, mass, massacres, rapes, abductions, and the vast influx of refugees. Many pages of the novel deal with communal issues. The reports of a possible partition of India into Hindu India and Muslim Pakistan, has led to riots that started in Sialkot on twenty-fourth of June. From this fierce background, the historical novelist goes on to paint the picture of the peaceful city, Sialkot, which was soon to be changed due to the partition. Sialkot, a city in which Hindus and Muslims breathed in harmony with love and affection is now the centre of religious hatred, violence and atrocities where there is no place for Hindus and Sikhs because "those who had stayed behind after the fifteenth of August had either been annihilated or converted to Islam; it was no city for the Hindus any longer." (148). It is the woolly thinking of Lala Kanshi Ram to stay in Sialkot after the partition. The tragic sense is shown through significant gestures and through noteworthy suggestions. Sialkot is the scene of frenzied activity after the announcement of the partition, "more than murders, it was the fires that were frightening and demoralizing." (105)

Not only fires but trains are also victims of violence. The events and characters that are portrayed in this novel could be taken to be the models of those that took place in many parts of north India at the time of partition. The novel captures the mindlessness of the communal violence with great objectivity in the portrayal of the situation before and after the massacres. The main victims of the communal riots were women. They were abducted, raped and brutally treated by the Muslim hooligans. They took a ghoulish delight in killing and raping Hindu women. It presents realistic scenes of the horrible condition in the refugee camp in Pakistan.

> "A number of abducted Hindu and Sikh women were in their custody. Many of the kidnapped women disappeared into private homes. A lone Muslim dragged a woman away, and kept her for his own exclusive use. Or he took her with the consent of other Muslims, converted her to Islam and got married to her. The rest were subjected to mass rape, at time in public places and in the presence of large gatherings. The rape was followed by other atrocities, chopping off the breasts, and even death. Many of the pregnant women had their wombs torn open. The survivors were retained for repeated rapes and humiliations, until they were parcelled out to decrepit wrecks—the aged, the left-over who couldn't find a wife, or those Muslims who wanted an additional wife. In the meantime more women were abducted and the cycle was repeated all over again." (258)

And all this is being done in the name of religion. The attacks of the Muslim fanatical mobs on Hindu refugees, is realistically presented by the novelist. The horrors and inhuman atrocities of the partition in the name of religion find powerful expression in *Azadi*. The author finds the attitude of the Muslims towards the Hindu women quite repugnant. They have not shown any mercy for the unfortunate and wretched women. The author emphasizes on the violent and unkind atmosphere in Sialkot where the atrocities are committed by the frenzied Muslims. The account of the parading of the naked Hindu women by Muslims at Narowal is an example of an abhorrent offense. Arun, who has been taken by Suraj Prakash to the market to watch this, is blunted at the sight of this squalor of man. The queer parade of naked Hindu women in Narowal is really grim and pathetic:

> "There were forty women, marching two abreast. Their ages varied from sixteen to thirty…They were all stark naked. Their heads were completely shaven; so were their armpits…The women walked awkwardly, looking only at the ground. They were all crying, though their eyes shed no tears. Their faces were formed into grimaces and they were sobbing. Their arms were free, but so badly had they been used, so wholly their spirits crushed, their morale shattered that none of them made any attempt to cover themselves with their hands…The bruises on their bodies showed they had been beaten and manhandled. Their masters walked beside them and if any of the women sagged or hung behind, they prodded her along with the whips they carried. At the head of the procession marched a single drummer with a flat drum, thumping heavily on it and announcing their arrival." (260-261)

The description of the naked women parade is really awful. It dramatizes the dehumanization of life and the collapse of all values. The passage highlights the harsh and shameful behaviour of the rioters. Later Arun comes to know about a similar parade of the Muslim women in Amritsar. The incidents that have taken place on both the sides of the newly formed borders of India and Pakistan are enough to prove that if religion can make a god of a man, it can also turn him into the worst kind of beast. The Muslims and the Hindus both blame each other for starting and planning the riots. However, the fact is that both sides have abducted, killed, shot, impaled, battered, tortured and raped. The statement of Barkat Ali clears the situation that:

> "Whatever is happening in Sialkot, things very much like that are happening on the other side too—let's make no mistake about it. It is not the collapse of Congress Muslims in Pakistan, apparently it is the collapse of Congress Hindus in India also. When refugees with stories of personal misfortunes land here, the politicians use them to their advantage to fan up further hatred." (118)

Lala Kanshi Ram and his family get a bolt from the blue, when the news of Arun's sister Madhu and her husband's death reaches to them. The strain must have been enormous, but Lala Kanshi Ram bore it well. He knows, "many parts of him had died but there were others still alive, forcefully and affirmatively alive, and he knew he was not defeated." (240) The characters in the novel are based upon the real people the authors knew or read about them. The character of Madhu is similar to Nahal's own sister, Kartar Devi who was killed with her husband by a hostile mob when she was coming to Sialkot from Wazirabad. Arun visits the railway station in search for her body but he comes across the heart-rending scene of dead bodies. Nahal gives a detail description of the scene:

> "The stench was unbearable as they approached the area. The four heaps were piled high, legs, and arms, and hands, and thighs, and feet. The fire consumed other parts of the bodies; it was the parts which had not fully burned that stood out. And there were the skulls. Again, dozens of them. Many lay face down, the others faced the sky, or looked sideways. Bare jaws, scooped out eye-sockets, gnashing teeth. Very often a skull cracked open with a popping noise, its bones disintegrating into the heap around. The dead had been removed from the train and dumped there without sentiment or concern. It so happened many of them had their arms around each other... and the eyes of one skull seemed to look into the eyes of another and send unspoken messages. For the other skull would nod, in a way saying it had quite understood." (158)

The author has used trivial characters to represent different phases of human behaviour during that tragedy released by the partition of the country. There is Gangu Mull, the husband of Bibi Amar Vati, who changes his religion and becomes Ghulam Muhammad so that he can take benefit of the large property of his wife. He wants to marry a Muslim girl. He does not care for his family and his wife who "looked crestfallen, confirmed as she was in the knowledge that the piece of charcoal she had been trying to pass off as a jewel all these years was nothing but a piece of coal." (239) The character of Gangu Mall shows that the Muslims of Pakistan force the Hindus to embrace Islam. There is no such incident that has been shown from the sides of the Hindus in India in the novel. In comparison with Gangu Mull, we have Niranjan Singh, a young Sikh who represents inflexible respect for religion. When he is asked to cut his long hair, he refuses and declares, "Loose your head, if needed be/ Don't lose your Sikh faith!" (215) The long hair is necessary for Sikh religion and it is very easy to recognize a Sikh by his turban and beard. So, many Sikhs cut their hair off though it is against their religion. But in case of Niranjan Singh no amount of coaxing or advice can make him change his mind. When he finds that he may be forced into doing that by the members of his family and well-wishers and he knows very well that his wife is expecting his child still he prefers to immolate himself rather than do what goes against his religion. Through this character, the author projects the plight of Sikhs at the time of partition. They were forced to do what their religion denies because a Sikh sporting his head gear was an easy target of attack by the Muslims. But somewhere he also presents the rigid and conservative outlook of the Sikhs towards their religion.

The partition of the sub-continent not only affected the geographical boundaries of the countries—India and Pakistan, but also the life and relations of people. The novel shows the impact of the partition in the relationship of love, marriage and friendship. The life-long friendship of Lala Kanshi Ram and Chaudhari Barkat Ali comes to an end when the former was forced to leave the city and country. The author has given a microscopic picture of their separation which is very pathetic. Barkat Ali has left his friend with a positive thought that "if not in our life-time, Insha-Allah in the life time of our children this folly will surely be undone."

He further says that "we are one people and religion cannot separate us from each other." (242)

The communal bitterness that is the result of the partition penetrates so deep in the lives of the people that such close friends as Arun and Munir too feel tension towards each other. But later, Arun and Munir also experience the pain of separation. Munir does not want to go back from the refugee camp where Lala Kanshi Ram has stayed with his family. The novel records lively and passionately the pain, trauma and sufferings of those who have to part from their kith and kin, friends and neighbours. Chaman Nahal's Azadi shows stark realism and basic human relationships in narratives admixing with conventional romantic love. The matrimonial relationship of Bibi Amar Vati and Gangu Mull has come to an end when Gangu Mull has changed his religion and left his wife. Arun loves the daughter of Barkat Ali, Nur and is ready to change his religion and wants to become a Muslim for her sake. The love story of Arun and Nur arouses emotional feelings in the atmosphere of hatred and violence. The love of Nur comes out in these words, "will I ever see you again? God alone knows why people are so full of hate. I wish they were not to part souls that loved each other. But I'll think of you till the day of my death." (231) But after partition, suddenly Arun becomes conscious about his Hindu identity. In his frustration and irritation, he asks, "Why should I become a Muslim? Why shouldn't you? That is, if you love me. Why shouldn't you become a Hindu?" (78) Although they love each other but they start to view others through their religious eyes. The influence of religion is shown in the pure and deep love of Arun and Nur that "ceases to be a private, personal affair, and in spite of them it comes to acquire communal or political overtones."(*Three Contemporary,* Dhawan, 72) Arun has lost his love because Nur is a Muslim girl. Again during the journey back to India, he goes through the same pain when his new-found beloved Chandini is kidnapped by the Muslim marauders during an attack on the refugee camp. Representatively the parting of the lovers, friends and husband-wife is connected with the partition of the nation. But Nahal has focused on another aspect of these relations that they are affected by the partition but not by communal violence. The love relationship of Arun-Nur, friendship of Arun-Munir and Lala Kanshi Ram-Chaudhari Barkat has remained true in their heart. The sweetness of their relations will always be in their hearts.

The torment of partition of the country and the communal riots that erupted were traumatic which left its imprints on the social order. The narrator has caught the beliefs and spirit of that time very efficiently. He has used his personal experiences to expose the pain and trauma of people during the time of partition. Lala Kanshi Ram mirrors the state of confusion, conflict and disorder which are faced by the millions of the Hindus and the Muslims. The novel unveils the fear of loss and anxiety to leave the place where one has been born and brought up. Lala Kanshi Ram is forced by his son, Arun and wife, Prabha Rani to leave Sialkot. But he is unhappy with the entire situation and about his loss. He weeps with sorrow when he thinks about his future. Scenes like this are neither exceptional nor the preserver of one particular community. Khushwant Singh has also treated the same kind of situation in his novel *Train to Pakistan* through the sentiments of Muslims who are forced to leave their small village Mano Majra where they are born and brought up with the feeling of brotherhood. Kanshi Ram is totally disheartened and frustrated. Lala Kanshi Ram does not want to leave Sialkot at any cost. He is ready to "become a Muslim to stay here, if need be." (111)

The novelist observes minutely the deep sorrow of the minorities and it is well expressed by the feelings of the protagonist, Lala Kanshi Ram:

> "But to leave Sialkot? Lala Kanshi Ram ran his hand over the wall of his room and something in him snapped. No, he couldn't just give it up. Behind these walls lay years of labour and hope. He was young though, he was only fifty, he could start a business somewhere else, in some town on the other side of the border. But could he? Could he, really...now wasn't that asking a little too much of a middle-aged man? And where precisely would he begin? In what city? How much capital did he have in cash? How early, at how short a notice, could he withdraw it from the bank? What of the shop—the grain stored there? How would he dispose of it? Would anyone give him any price for it in such times?" (110)

The inner confusion of Lala Kanshi Ram is well interpreted by the author. The author describes the small and minute happenings on a very large and wide scale. The novel is full of such extracts which express the touching emotional state of characters bit by bit and create the whole environment. The scene is very pathetic when Prabha Rani and Arun pack their luggage and Lala Kanshi Ram "watched them with the immense tightening of the heart. They were stripping the walls bare, and Lala Kanshi Ram felt they were stripping his flesh from his body. The bone was showing—whichever way he turned." (121)

These lines reflects Nahal's pain and longing for his homeland in the words of Lala Kanshi Ram. The novelist uses many colourful and peculiar characters to express the agony, wretchedness and regret of the entire atmosphere in the novel. Before leaving for the camp, Lala Kanshi Ram desires for peace and prosperity from the bottom of his heart. He is ready "to forgive the English and the Muslims all their sins—if only he could return. Return and die here and be cremated by the sides of the river Aik. He shivered at the luxury of the thought." (125) The thought expresses the deep love and affection of Lala Kanshi Ram towards his land of birth. S.C. Singh remarks at this situation, "The politicians made Lala Kanshi Ram a nowhere man, a castaway along with a number of people as houseless wretches and refugees. In the name of "Azadi" they played different roles and partitioned India into two nations—India and Pakistan." (*Indian Writing,* Chakravarty, 8)

The agony of leaving the places inhabited by generations, the torment of those believers who got removed from their places of worship and the harrowing experiences of those uncountable people who boarded trains thinking they would be transported to the realization of their dreams but of whom not a man, woman or child survived the journey is indeed pathetic. Needless to say, the novel is about the horrifying and gruesome incidents of the partition but it also presents the expansive vision of the novelist. Lala Kanshi Ram after reaching Amritsar moves to Delhi. During that course of journey, he has come across similar scenes and happenings which he saw in Pakistan. He is unable to understand the difference between the Hindus of India and Muslims of Pakistan. The incidents which only reflect the feeling of pity, repugnance, loathing, and shame are common on either side of the border. Nahal does not impeach any particular party or community. He finds both the Hindus and the Muslims equally responsible for the inhuman deeds. Lala Kanshi Ram who hates Muslims for their cruel and violent activities is forced to think about the conduct of his own community. While moving from the city of Kurukshetra, he said, "I have ceased to hate... I can't hate the Muslims anymore." (298) The novelist has shown different shades of the character of the protagonist, Lala Kanshi Ram. He "takes a stance which clearly demonstrates his freedom from commitment to anything except love, compassion and tolerance which alone makes political freedom more meaningful." (*Indian English,* Prasad, 89) The novelist has again shown the teaching of Gandhiji to hate the sin not the sinner through his hero, Lala Kanshi Ram who is a true follower of Gandhiji. He blames both the communities equally for this ghoulish drama and Lala Kanshi Ram says, "We have sinned as much. We need their forgiveness!' (300)

This quality of Lala Kanshi Ram stands him out among all the heroes of other partition novels. The novelist has introduced the element of spiritualism and the recommendation of renewal in the middle of the genocide. The train of butchered Muslims on one side represents the devastation and the demolition. On the other side, the newly born baby of Isher Kaur in the train epitomizes the hope for the future. The novel indicates the cycle of the world as depicted in the Vedas. The comment of A.N. Dwivedi is remarkable:

"As if these hints are not enough, a baby is born in the train—a visible symbol that crystallises much of what this novel stands for—life, love compassion, hope. The train passes through Kurukshetra which subtly reminds the reader of the necessity of action preached there by a great *Yogi* a few thousand years ago. To be meaningful, however, action has got to be at the level of the individual to each his own Kurukshetra." (*Studies in*, Dwievedi, 324)

Azadi focuses mainly on the partition and also clarifies the factors leading to partition and the grisly aftermath. It shows the pathetic and miserable conditions of the refugees which creates a new class of minorities. Kanshi Ram wanted to live a life of peace and love. The novel displays the misery of the refugees from Pakistan in India. They find no room, the houses of their relatives in India are overcrowded, the trains going to Pakistan are derailed and thousands of Muslims butchered mercilessly. Lala Kanshi Ram and other refugees like him have faced every difficulty with the only hope that at least his people understand his pain and will welcome him in India. But he gets a shock when he comes to know that in Delhi local people dislike the refugees. He gets another blow when the Area Custodian Officer demands one thousand rupees for giving a flat, an amount which he cannot afford. The narrator exposes the cruel behaviour of the custodian officers as they "drunk with the power of their office, they were impatient and intolerant— with most of the refugees." (307) The novelist highlights the depressed and pitiable condition of Lala Kanshi Ram in a very realistic manner. His happy and calm life is rudely shattered and uprooted due to the tumultuous event of the partition. He is unhappy at the partition of India and his indignation has been very realistically expressed in *Azadi*. Lala Kanshi Ram who is so brave and courageous that despite all his own struggles and after losing his daughter and son-in-law; he supports his friends and family in Pakistan but he feels defeated and rancorous by people of his own community in his own country. He weeps bitterly in the Rehabilitation office and that too in his country India, not in Pakistan. K.K. Sharma rightly says:

> "Nahal portrays effectively a little world of these people—their placid, easy and happy lives before the partition, their terrible misfortunes during the undeclared civil war and their completely changed lives after the storm is over. Obviously, the novelist fully succeeds in delineating the true dimensions of the events that accompanied the partition, showing their physical and psychological impacts on human life." (*Exploration in*, Dhawan, 47)

The sarcasm of the situation is remarkably stated by the author. The author reflects on the problem which refugees faced at that time which was the tension between refugees and the local residents. Lala Kanshi Ram is a nowhere man; he reveals that he has just woken from a bad dream to worse reality and "never before in his life had he felt so exposed, so naked, so defenceless." (309) The author observes the miserable condition of Lala Kanshi Ram and his family very painstakingly.

The novel, *Azadi* highlights not only the immediate results of the partition but the far-reaching effect of the partition on the lives of refugees. Nahal in his novel, brings out not only the irremediable losses but also the loss of personality and identity. Kanshi Ram was a prosperous person and a well-known whole-sale grain merchant in Sialkot. He had a noble and esteemed image in society but in India, he becomes a refugee who is a hapless and hopeless person. He has lost his identity and that is why he is struggling just for 'a name for himself once again—not fame, just a name.' (310) This brings the final catastrophe with complete loss of individuality and there starts a quest for new identity for Lala Kanshi Ram. At that time, both the communities had gone through the same kind of situation. The condition on the other side of the border was the same during and after the partition. The Muslims, who had left India for Pakistan, did not receive any welcome and were considered as 'outsider' or 'Mujahir' which means refugee. They had also struggled to settle there again. The inner conflicts and rigidities also increased between the incoming refugees and the local residents in Pakistan. The refugees of Pakistan had also gone through the same pain. Attia Hosain reflects on the problem of 'loss of identity' on the other side of the border in a similar manner in her novel through the character of Saleem who has left India for his 'neo-paradise', Pakistan. But he has not felt like home in Pakistan. He belonged to a very high-class family in India but he has lost his identity in Pakistan among his own people.

The emotional trauma which has been faced by refugees is well voiced in the novel. The novel also presents the psychosomatic and self-induced influence of the partition which results in the loss of communication. It projects the problem of alienation and discrimination suffered by refugees in India. Lala Kanshi Ram and his family suffer alienation. They suffer from a loss of communication and "not being able to fathom their minds and feeling restless about it. Not being able to talk to each other and feeling guilty about it... A sadness weighed on their hearts, and each felt stifled, crushed." (327) The element of alienation is thus well communicated in the novel. This situation is a result of disaster, muddle, struggle and grief faced by millions who go through the harrowing experiences of the partition. Perhaps, the most important question which has not been asked by the other writers but only by Chaman Nahal is --what was the fault of the millions like him who were removed from their roots?

> "The complete loss of contact and communication throws them into a vortex of complete isolation and alienation, and making each a prisoner of his own single self. This process of isolation, whether expansive or narrow, is productive of confusion, conflict and sorrow unleashed by partition tragedy." *(Partition Perspectives*, Rao, 59)

Azadi is different from other partition novels because of its underlying optimism. The novel ends with a sadly depleted family trying to begin life anew. Like Attia Hosain, Nahal also has an optimistic outlook—to make a fresh start after crossing all hurdles. Lala Kanshi Ram has received so many thunderbolts and trauma that now he stops wearing the turban because, "a turban was a sign of respect, of dignity. He had no dignity left. He now wore a forage cap. Or he sat bare-headed, advertising his humble position to the world." (323)The reaction of Lala Kanshi Ram is the result of the situation that he has faced after reaching India. He has also tried to meet Nehru but in vain. The novel moves towards a new self-awareness. Nahal has amply and adequately illustrated this point of view in *Azadi*. He has adopted a positive approach through his characters Lala Kanshi Ram, Arun and Sunanda who try to settle down again after insurmountable obstacles. The values which appear in the novel are benevolence, generosity and tolerance, abiding human love and respect for the lowly and the downtrodden. Lala Kanshi Ram has taken the responsibility of Bibi AmarVati and Sunanda after both the ladies lose their menfolk. Lala Kanshi Ram does not give up his efforts and ultimately he finds a refugee flat which is not very good but 'after about four months of irregular living under canvas, they found this a luxury.'(314)

The life of living under a canvas in a refugee camp is not easy to bear for him, when "the wind that blew non-stop through those tents, it had driven holes through his body. He wanted walls around himself and doors and he wanted a bed to lie on and clean sheets and he wanted Prabha Rani to be alone with him." (310)

The novel *Azadi* has not shown any element of the excitement, energy and enthusiasm like the other novels about the partition, such as Khushwant Singh's *Train to Pakistan* and Manohar Malgonkar's *A Bend in the Ganges*. Lala Kanshi Ram does not sacrifice his life in Jugga's style in *Train to Pakistan*. Lala Kanshi Ram loses all that of which he was proud in his life. He has lost every bright aspect of his life; the grace and glory all have vanished. He is forced to live in utter dejection and hopelessness.

The novelist shows the positive energy and optimistic approach through Sunanda's sewing machine which symbolises a new inspiration and hope for future. The novelist gives the message that whatever happens, life goes on. The character of Sunanda is very strong because it shows her courage to move forward even after losing her husband and being brutally raped by a Muslim army officer. After facing all the hurdles of life, she takes her first step towards life and starts stitching clothes as well as her fate for her children, "The machine went whirring on, its wheel turning fast and its needle moving up and down, murmuring and sewing through the cloth." (327)

The whirling of Sunanda's machine denotes the ineffectiveness of revulsion that refugees got from people of India and Pakistan. Kanshi Ram too exposes the freedom of mind and spirit that is the result of freedom of the nation. The comment of Bhasker Rao is remarkable about Sunanda and Kanshi Ram:

> "The initiative now passes into the hands of the individual. She is no longer a passive victim but can stitch out her own destiny. Love and creative action as evidenced in the lives of Kanshi Ram and Sunanda respectively are all the supreme values which form the moving drama of violence and malevolence. Without love collective action is merely compulsion, breeding antagonism and fear, from which arises private and social conflicts. Through self-knowledge alone is there freedom from bondage, and this freedom is devoid of all beliefs, all ideologies." (*(Partition Perspectives*, Rao, 59)

Azadi is the manifestation of the gory details of the partition of the sub-continent. It seizes the spirit of that time robustly. The paramount quality of the novel lies in its powerful delineation of the traumatic experiences of ordinary men and women in the course of the unhappy event. The Hindus, the Sikhs and the Muslims, all the communities indulged in bestiality and savagery. But the accent falls on love, harmony and friendliness in place of hatred, fear and violence. Even in this darkness the light of humanity and godliness was not completely extinguished. Many Muslims were saved by the Hindus and Sikhs in India and the same gentleness and kindness was shown by the Muslims in Pakistan. Nahal shows the cruelty as well as the humanity of human nature on both sides of the border.

Azadi is a moving tale of the agony and ecstasy of partition which is expressed effectively through the tragedy of Kanshi Ram, his family and friends. The novelist pulls the attention of readers towards political tension, psychological impact, emotional transmutation as well as human values. Nahal has brilliantly described every event of partition which throws light on the inner tension of the situation. The whole narrative is based on the views and observation of Lala Kanshi Ram and Arun. The pain of leaving the place, home and kith and kin is shown by Lala Kanshi Ram. He reflects on the problem of bread and butter and resettlement in a new place and struggle for home. His anxiety and frustration is justifiable for as the head of the family he wants to give all comforts but is incapable to do so. Meticulous attention to details and first-hand knowledge of the life of the characters enable Nahal to make the plight of the refugees real to the reader. On the other hand, Arun reflects on the thoughts and dynamism of the young generation. Through his point of view, Nahal stresses on the pain of leaving love and friends. The relationship of Arun-Nur and Arun-Chandini present the element of love. The novel shows the maturing of Arun, but the justification of his love, first for Nur, the Muslim girl left behind in Pakistan, and then for Chandini, a low-caste girl who is abducted on the way to India, is not as gripping as the rest of the novel. The author observes many characters through Arun's eyes. He is a witness to the blood-curdling scene of the rape of beautiful Sunanda and his killing of the rapist Rahmat Ullah Khan. The murder of Rahmat Ullah Khan is the result of Arun's frustration of losing his home, his love and his sister. With the help of these two characters, Lala Kanshi Ram and Arun, the novelist brings out the problem related to society, political, moral and ethical. As O.P. Mathur reckons:

> "Chaman Nahal is not a rebel against life or one who believes that it means nothing. He is a determined and sturdy affirmationist whose novels reveal a sound commitment to moral values, to right action, to life itself. The background may be domestic, inter-cultural or the movement of history, but they are all irradiated with the emotional and spiritual luminosity of man, the potentiality of his being. His novels are celebrations of life and those of its qualities which give it meaning and significance." (*Modern English,* Mathur, 145)

Nahal focuses on the traumatic experiences of different characters that have gone through violence, brutality, bloodshed, rape, arson and have been deceived by their own men. The author highlights their pain through the reaction of Arun and Lala Kanshi Ram which gives a strong base to the novel. The novel provides the statistics and incidents to understand the people and true meaning of humanity. It maintains a humorous as well as tragic tone. It manifests varying shades of the partition tragedy through the major and minor characters, comprehending the trauma and catastrophe of the partition in terms of the dislocation, communal discord, disgrace and mortifications that have to be endured by the people driven to find a new home and a new identity. It stresses on the necessity and inevitability of settlement and action. It expects the victims to move ahead while defeating the disasters of the partition. Nahal died a natural death on 29 November 2013. He was 86. *Azadi*, does not convey the message of dejection and distrust. It clearly shows the triumph of human values and the courage and fortitude of man in overcoming difficulties and surviving against all odds.

Works Cited

Bhatta, S.C. "A Review on Azadi", The Literary Criterion, Vol. XII, Nos. 2-3, 1976.

Dwievedi A.N. (Ed), "The novels of Chaman Nahal—A Penultimate View", *Studies in Contemporary Indian Fiction in English.* Allahabad: Kitab Mahal, 1987.

Dhawan, R.K. *Three Contemporary Novelists.* New Delhi: Classical Publishing Company, 1985.

Dhawan, R.K. (Ed.), "Artist as historian" *Three Contemporary Novelists.* New Delhi: Classical Publishing Company, 1985.

Mathur, O.P. "Chaman Nahal", *Indian English Novelists: an anthology of critical essays* (Ed.) Madhusudan Prasad. New Delhi: Sterling Publishers, 1982.

Nahal, Chaman.*Azadi.* New Delhi: orient Paperback, 1975, (All the subsequent references given in the parenthesis are from this edition)

Nahal, Chaman "Writing A Historical Novel", *Three Contemporary Novelists* (Ed.) R.K. Dhawan. New Delhi: Classical Publishing Company, 1985.

Naiker, Basavaraj. "The Trauma of the Partition in *Azadi"Modern Indian Writing in English: Critical Perception, Vol1.*(Ed.) N.D.R. Chandra.New Delhi: Sarup & Sons, 2004.

Jha, Rama. Review of Azadi, in Indian Literature, Vol. XXI/5(1978) 114.

Ramamurti, K.S. "Azadi—Point of view as Technique," *Three Contemporary Novelist*, Ed. R.K. Dhawan. New Delhi: Classical Publishing Company, 1985.

Rao, V. Pala Prasad. *"India-Pakistan: Partition Perspectives in Indo-English Novels.* New Delhi: Discovering Publishing House, 2004.

Sharma, K.K. "The 1947 Upheavel and the Indian English Novel" *Exploration in Modern Indo-English Fiction* (Ed.) R.K. Dhawan. New Delhi: Classical Publishing Company, 1985.

Singh, S.C. "Chaman Nahal's Azadi: An Appraisal" *Indian writing in English: perspectives* (Ed.) Joya Chakravarty. New Delhi: Atlantic Publishers and Distributers, 2003.

Tak, A. H. "Historiographic Metafiction and Chaman Nahal's Azadi: An Appraisal" *Akademi Awarded Novels in English: Millennium Responses*, Ed. Mithilesh K. Pandey. New Delhi: Sarup & Sons, 2003), 110

ICE-CANDY-MAN

Ice-Candy Man (1988) is written by a woman novelist from Pakistan, Bapsi Sidhwa. It is the only novel written on the theme of the Partition by a Parsi who does not belong to either of the two communities which perpetrated havoc on each other. It is a recent and significant novel which presents the perspectives about the partition of the subcontinent from the Pakistani point of view. It is one of the first avant-garde works to appeal to a wide audience. The novel has also been presented in the form of the film 'Earth 1947', which was directed by the Indian director Deepa Mehta. The movie showcases the havoc and pandemonium of the partition, described by the writer in the novel. The motion picture was nominated for the 72nd Academy Award for Best Foreign Film in 2000.

The novel presents the partition as a means of diffusion of disharmony which resulted in fury, commotion and turmoil. The novel encapsulates every emotion and suffering of people during the partition. It illustrates the pains of the sub-continent during the partition which was a crucial time in the history of India and Pakistan. The novelist examines the unremitting reasons of the partition as the consequences of communal cacophony. *Ice Candy Man* portrays the vivid images of communal harmony among the three communities but rumours introduce the poison of discord and hatred in the city. It traces the communal discord that occurred at the time of the independence. The author depicts the horror of the Partition with tear-jerking truth. The emotional effects of the partition on the lives of people are shown through various aspects in the novel. The novel has also Parsi consideration through which the tragic and dreadful event is depicted. The book throws light on how the socio-political and religious factors destroy the harmonious environment of Lahore.

The novel has a gripping story with a forceful theme. The partition theme influenced the novelist to such an extent that her other two novels *The Crow Eaters* and *The Pakistani Bride* are also imbued with the same theme. The theme of the novel *Ice Candy Man* is not traditional but modern. The novel is divided into 32 chapters. Unlike Chaman Nahal, Bapsi Sidhwa uses the single person narrative technique and the narrator is an eight-years-old Parsi girl, Lenny. Lenny narrates the whole incident in the same way as Laila, in *Sunlight on a Broken Column* and throws light on the factors which lead to the partition. The novelist delivers the novel with tremendous wit and verve. Bapsi Sidhwa gives the touch of satire and metaphor in the novel to make it more interesting and meaningful. It provides an equal amount of humour and tragedy also. First published under the name of *Ice-Candy-Man* in 1988, the title was changed to *Cracking India* in 1991. The former title of the novel was after a character, a Muslim street vendor but the new title exposes the theme and political condition of the partition of the sub-continent. P.D. Nimsarkar comments:

"The title 'Cracking India' straightway relates the history of the partition and politics whereas 'Ice Candy Man' tells about an individual person heading a combination of communal strands. The novel is a powerful discourse on the multiple histories, of nations, of communities and of individuals." (*Contemporary Fiction,* Nimsarkar, 78)

The novel progresses with the events and periodic provisions but it is fragmented in structure and does not give the textual consistency. Sidhwa somewhere uses pictorial language with remarkable facts in order to arouse interest in the readers. The novel is in the form of fictional autobiography as the author uses her own childhood experiences to describe the horrors of the Partition. It reflects the creative craftsmanship and innovative brilliance of Sidhwa's talent. She wonderfully portrays the characters with a shrewd vision into human nature and psyche. The characters are complete and based on reality. They aptly express their emotions and frustration. Sidhwa uses some Urdu words in the novel to give the impact of Muslim culture and also highlights the fact that the languages used by the characters are Urdu and Punjabi. The novel is written in the present tense so that it helps the novelist to create a reasonable and rational picture of the time of the partition.

Sidhwa has sharply and deftly maintained her role as a preserver of culture. She is a folk historian and mythmaker. Sidhwa depicts each and every aspect of Parsi life through the novel. She denotes the migratory nature of her community, their flexibility, peculiarity, ethnic customs, rituals and religious beliefs. While providing these facts, she is very particular with her own details and acquaintances. She explains the traditional story of arrival of the Parsees from Iran to the subcontinent in the 8th century. The novel shows the fact that the Parsees have made persevering efforts to absorb themselves into Indian culture. But during the partition the assiduous efforts of the Parsees are in vain when they face the warning of extinction. The novel also focuses on one of the characteristics of the Parsi community and that is their loyalty for the country of their residence. Even during the partition, the Hindus, Muslims and Sikhs migrated on both sides of the border but the Parsees did not leave the country neither in India nor in Pakistan. The Parsi community was not under attack by the major community of any of the countries at the time of the partition. The novelist harps on this fact when communal Muslims gather in Lenny's house and try to harm them. Imam Din, the cook says, "there are no Hindus here......the Sethis are Parsees. I serve them. Sethis is a Parsee name too." (Ice.., Sidhwa, 180) The novel presents the customs and religious practices of Parsees like their worship place and the Fire Temple. Bapsi Sidhwa candidly expresses the lonesomeness and unfriendliness from which her community suffers. The author wants the narration to be free from racial and religious bias, so she portrays the central character of the novel, Lenny as an intelligent and bright eight-years-old Parsi girl. She is helpless and lame like Sidhwa herself because of polio in one leg. The author uses her weakness and vulnerability as her strength and presents it through the character of Lenny. The background of the novel is set in Lahore. The characters are set according to the event. The novel opens with the verse of Iqbal from his poem 'Complaint to God'. The narrator introduces the child-narrator Lenny with the poem. She uses the memories of Lenny to expose the anguish and agony of the Partition. Her narration starts in her fifth year and ends after her eighth birthday. The communal harmony and discord between the Hindus and Muslims are presented through the child narrator Lenny. Sidhwa endeavors to create logic from the ridiculous events of the Partition. The central part of the narration shows the growth of Lenny and her arousing interest towards the grown-up world with the ambience of the Partition. Lenny through her observation feels the pain of the calamitous event that tears her world apart. The idea of the child narrator helps the author to justify the historical moment as appalling and horrendous. Priyamvada Gopal rightly remarks:

> "The device of a handicapped Parsi child narrator ('Lame Lenny') allows Sidhwa to craft a self-consciously marginalized and innocent perspective on the horrors of the time, although a knowing authorial voice intrudes far too often. Set in Lahore in the 1940s, *Ice-Candy-Man* manages to tell a compelling story of a life where the joys and jollities of an idyllic childhood carry on uneasily next to the chilling cruelties of the time." (*Nation, History,* Priyamavada Gopal, 75)

The narrator belongs to the minor community of Parsees as expressed by Lenny, "Godmother, slave sister, electric aunt and my nuclear family are reduced to irrelevant nomenclatures. We are Parsee." (94) In the beginning, the novel shows the evasive approach of the Parsi community towards the partition. The Parsees remain neutral during the tumultuous events of the partition and that gives a chance to Lenny to present varied perspectives and the different philosophies of people living in Lahore and in other nearby localities. Lenny does not belong to any of the communities who suffer in the partition. This is the brightest aspect of the novel that gives strength to the theme. The Parses are loyal towards the British government but they are frightened and anxious about the thought of the Partition of the sub-continent, therefore they are perplexed as to which community they should support. Col. Bharucha, the Parsis doctor and the President of the Parsi speaks with concern and warning:

> "There may be not one but two or even three new nations! And the Parses might find themselves championing the wrong side—if they don't look before they leap! If we are stuck with the Hindus, they'll swipe our business from under our noses, and sell our grandfathers in the bargain: if we are stuck with the Muslims, they'll convert us by the sword! And God help us if we're stuck with the Sikhs!" (37)

To make things better Col. Bharucha suggests that they should be neutral, "Let whoever wishes rule! Hindu, Muslim, Sikh, Christian! We will abide by the rules of their land!" (39) The novel reflects the fact that the common man of any community is neutral and does not want to be involved in the politics of the country, but is persuaded by the religious and political differences of the country to be a party to the communal riots.

The novelist brilliantly describes the psychosomatic impact of the partition with the help of a child. Lenny does not understand the root meaning of the partition but she is affected by the surrounding atmosphere and sensitively and innocently asks, "Can one break a country? And what happens if they break it where our house is? Or crack it further up on Warris Road? How will I ever get to Godmother's then?" (92) The uprootedness of the partition is well exposed by Lenny when she tears her doll into two parts after she has seen the condition of fallen women and heard their screams. There is a feeling of uncertainty and sense of loss in Lenny who with her brother Adi roves through the Queen's Garden for known faces and associates, "Adi and I wander from group to group peering into faces beneath white skull-caps and above ascetic breads.... I feel uneasy. Like Hamida I do not fit. I know we will not find familiar faces here" (237). Lenny's story "takes the form of narrating the independence and birth of nations with all its illegitimate undertones and bourgeois betrayals." (En-Gendering.., Ray,137)The novel contains a cast of characters from all communities -- Hindus, Muslims, Christians, Sikhs and Parsees. It gives a chance to the author to present the catastrophic events in a wide canvas. Sidhwa does not seem interested in formal rules and small details. She presents the multiple perspectives of partition with the help of the characters who are affected in the Partition. The characters and their actions represent meticulous behaviour and background which has relation with their ethics, religion or politics. Lenny describes how her friends and neighbours become helpless and ineffective in front of mass fury.

The novel has a female standpoint as well. It keeps alive the curiosity and attention of the readers at the personal and political levels. The Centre of Lenny's world is her eighteen-year-old Hindu Ayah, Shanta. The author paints the character of the Ayah with a different mind-set. She is vivacious and friendly and is emblematic of female liveliness. Lenny is not affected by the social and political instability but is shocked when she suffers the loss of her Ayah. As Jill Didur suggests:

> "Lenny's 'education of desire' in her close relationship with Ayah takes her out of the confines of the bourgeois Parsi community and exposes her to the heterogeneity of socio-cultural perspectives that leads her to question dominant interpretations of history. Her autobiographical mode of writing indicates that, even as an adult, she continues to question and challenge these things and to consider her own complicity in their transparency." (Unsettling..., Didur, 93)

The narrator frequently stresses on the sexual charm of the Ayah. Lenny notices that, "Holy men, masked in piety, shove aside their pretences to ogle her with lust. Hawkers, cart- drivers, cooks, coolies and cyclists turn their heads as she passes...." (3) She has a lot of admirers of different communities and among them one is the Ice-candy-man. The amorous glances of the Ayah's admirers awaken her to sexuality and infatuation. In the beginning, she is a servant of a comfortable Parsee family but the partition has changed her life and she becomes a dancing girl and a prostitute. She is exploited and subjugated. The reason of her suffering is that she is a member of the minority community of the region and she "is a representative of the victimization sprung from the partition. The communal collision and place of woman in the patriarchal society, the historic trap has been revisited by using Ayah, caught in a flirting whirl with men."(Contemporary, Nimsarkar, 79) Sidhwa exposes the cruel fact of the partition through the character of the Ayah that women are the worst sufferers in the entire event. The traumatic experience leaves Ayah spiritually dead when she replies, "I am past that. I am not alive." (262) The women, during communal violence, are used as an article of trade and amusement. They are shown as being browbeaten and demoralized. The men have taken revenge by exploiting and oppressing the women. They show their power and pleasure by disobeying the privileges of women. Women have to bear the burden of the erroneous doings of men. Like Ayah, Hamida is also the prey of men's brutality. The character of Hamida is the representative of those women who are not accepted by their families because they are kidnapped and dishonoured. They are sent to a prostitute market or rehabilitation centres. But they cannot lead a normal life and face other kind of insensitive and inhuman behaviours. Sidhwa effectively establishes how Partition has affected the two nations in general and women in particular. Like Bapsi Sidhwa, Chaman Nahal also focuses on the pathetic condition of women during the partition. He mentions the cruelties of men on women through different ways like rape in public places, gang rape, parade of naked women and chopping of breasts etc. Sidhwa shows this violent and aggressive behaviour of men through the Ayah who represents many of the others like her. Both the authors deliberately provide the details of the incidents that mirror society and prove that man can also change into a beast.

The novel Ice-Candy-Man provides a significant dealing of a gynocentric view. It presents the feminine essence and experiences with a unique vision. If Sidhwa shows the miserable and shattered woman like Ayah she also focuses on the strength of women by sketching the character of the Godmother and Lenny's mother. Thesewomen characters are aware and confident of their individuality. They cannot be easily conquered. The character of the Godmother is the source of energy and comfort in the novel. She is a social worker and an influential lady who helps everyone. She has a reliable social network through which she gathers all latest news and information about everyone. She represents the character of strong and influential women among the British. She helps the Ayah to get out of the Hiramandi, the area of prostitutes and sends her to Amritsar where her relatives live. The character of the God-mother is autobiographical because the author mentions an incident in her interview when Sidhwa herself helped a girl in adversity. The novel throws light on the strength of women through different characters including Lenny's mother and her aunt who help kidnapped women in leaving Lahore safely and send them to their relatives or in Recovered Women's Camps. In order to help these women, Lenny's mother provides job opportunity to Hamida so that she can confidently start a new life. Lenny's relatives help the fallen women and the Muslim refugees by providing food and shelter to them. Lenny is close to women who are tough, audacious and adoring. The women characters affirm their autonomous selfhood and exhibit capability of assuming new roles and responsibilities. They also expose the patriarchal biases present in the contemporary social perceptions. Sidhwa recalls the chilling shrieks and moans of recovered women at the time. The novel is written with the considerable vigour of women characters and more than ever Parsi women who show their strong points in many places of the book. The impact of the Partition is understood by the novelist who gives a glimpse of the fallen women and refugees. The author undoubtedly does not show any power or potency in male characters. In comparison to female characters, male characters are lethargic and indolent. They do not present any moral ethics like the female characters. The male characters especially the Ice-Candy man is responsible for spreading destruction and violence and the suffering of the women. As Chelva Kanaganayakam observes, "characters like Lenny's father, Old husband and even Manek Mody are relatively insignificant in relation to Godmother and even Mother. And the little that is mentioned of Lenny's father is hardly complimentary." (Parsi Fiction, Kapadia & Dhawan, 43) In this way the novelist again establishes the impact of the female characters in the novel and presents them as redeemers and liberators.

The author very competently connects thechanging pattern of communal relationswith the theme of the novel through Lenny's first visit with Imam Din to Pir Pindo, a Muslim village thirty miles east of Lahore, where she has her first experience of rural life. Lenny observes the good relations amongst the Hindus, Muslims and Sikhs. All of them are sitting together and discussing the communal tension in the city. The communal harmony inPir Pindo is so profound that the members of both the communities are ready to sacrifice even their lives for protecting each other, "if need be, we'll protect our Muslim brothers with our lives!" (56)

There is a mutual understanding between the Sikhs and Muslims. They understand the need of each other and respect the feeling of brotherhood among them. The novelist brings out the feelings and emotions of characters efficiently because "a mere story is not the point of fiction; people and emotions are what's important." (Review, Narayan)

The elders of the village like the Sikh Granthi and the village Mullah are the stalwarts of communal amity, "Brother, our villages come from the same racial stock. Muslim or Sikh, we are basically Jats. We are brothers. How can we fight each other?" (56) The novel shows the difference in perspective of people of village and city, in the words of the Chaudhry of Pir Pindo,

> "But our relationships with the Hindus are boundby strong ties. The city folk can afford to fight we can't. We are dependent on each other: bound by our toil; by Mandi prices set by the Banyas-they're our common enemy-those city Hindus. To us villagers, what does it matter if a peasant is a Hindu, or a Muslim, or a Sikh?" (56)

The conversation reveals the internal problem of the peasants who are not concerned about the partition of India or the communal riots prevailing in the country but with the Hindu money-lenders, the Baniyas. The novel gives the feeling that rural Punjab is still free from communal hatred but the communal discord between the two communities in the cities is spreading rapidly, ready to destroy the peace of the village. Here, Pir Pindo and the adjoining village can be compared with Mano Majra of *Train to Pakistan* where there is peace and brotherhood to such an extent that even Sikhs are ready to fight for the Muslims. But the train from Pakistan reaches Mano Majra and destroys the harmonious environment of the village. Both the novelists focus on the same point that at this stage of the history of the sub-continent, communal relations between the rural communities was still harmonious and amicable. Like Sidhwa, Khushwant Singh also focuses on the Sikh-Muslim unity and cordial relations in his novel. He blames Indian leaders and the British for the partition. In the same way, Sidhwa presents her views through the character of the Inspector General Mr. Rogers who expresses the view that the differences between the Congress under the leadership of Nehru and the Muslim League under Jinnah are pushing India towards the Partition. He feels that it is the English who are the root cause of flaming the hatred between the two communities. The novelist demonstrates the pattern of communal discord that occurred at the time of partition from complete harmony to total frenzy and chaos. During her first visit to Dera Tek Singh, Lenny witnesses the Muslim and Sikh unity and their concern over the current situation. But on her second visit she observes the suspicion and animosity in the village. Lenny's nightmare also exposes the horrible and dreadful situation at the time of partition.

The main part of the novel shows the element of the disintegration. The Ayah is the center of the novel and all the events revolve around her including the Second World War, freedom struggle of India and the partition of the subcontinent. The character of the Ayah is emblematic with India and members of her circle who are also her admirers match up to the different religion of the sub-continent. She treats everyone equally without any favoritism. She represents India and her admirers signify the different cultures of India. The Ayah's group is together even when the fire of communal discord reaches Lahore and that shows an image of the freedom struggle where the people of all the religions fight against the common enemy, the British. A similar symbol of the unity of Indian religions is presented by the visitors to the Queen's Park where initially men of all religions and creed meet and spend time together but with the proximity of Partition, the same Park presents a picture of different religious groups keeping away from one another's company. With the partition looming large the admirers of Ayah become conscious of their communal identities. The novel highlights the fact that the members belonging to the various communities of India become mindful of their individual identity but at the cost of composite culture that evolved after centuries. Slowly and gradually it also affects the Ayah's group. Ayah's attraction and sensuousness cannot keep the circle intact. The admirers and friends of Ayah meet less frequently at the Queen's Park and more at the Wrestler's Restaurant. Through this geographical shift the novelist exposes the changes in the air which is an intuition of the occurrence of the communal discord. The novel establishes the deterioration of the characters through Ayah's friends who become her assailants. Asghar Ali Engineer opines, "A minority always and somewhat naturally, fears that it will be dominated by the majority community and that it will be denied proper share in power on the one hand, and on the other, its religio-cultural tradition will come underattack." (*Communalism,* Engineer, 28)

Ice Candy Man also delineates the theme of dislodgment and displacement. It exposes the cruel reality of the partition through the estimation of the population of the refugees.

> "Instead wave upon scruffy wave of Muslim refugees flood Lahoreand the Punjab west of Lahore. Within three months seven million Muslims and five million Hindus and Sikhs are uprooted in the largest and most terrible exchange

of population known to history. The Punjab has been divided by the icy card-sharks dealing out the land and village by village, city by city, wheeling and dealing and doling out favours." (159)

The novel highlights the dilemma of the people of the minority community who are in confusion of staying back or migrating and they find their safety in migration but they are opposing the idea of migration or leaving everything behind, "where can the scared Muslim villagers go? There are millions of themhow can they abandon their ancestor's graves, every inch of land they own, their other kin? How will they ever hold up their heads again. Where will they go? No, he says, I have seen for myself; they cannot throw Mussalmans out!" (109) During the partition, almost all the people of India especially the people of Punjab were faced with such quandary. They could not grasp the severity of the situation. They were not expecting to be uprooted and dislocated. Here, the thought process of the Muslims is reminiscent of the character of Lala Kanshi Ram in *Azadi*, who is in confusion when he is forced to leave Sialkot:

"But to leave Sialkot? Lala Kanshi Ram ran his hand over the wall of his room and something in him snapped. No, no he couldn't just give it up. Behind these walls lay years of labour and hope.he could start a business somewhere else, in some town on the other side of the border. But could he? Could he, really...now wasn't that asking a little too much of a middle-aged man? And where precisely would he begin? In what city?" (*Azadi*, Chaman Nahal, 110)

Home is the safest place for everybody and suddenly if they are informed that this is not their home, people cannot overcome the shock and the pain of being uprooted. The authors of both the novels highlight the fact that neither Hindus nor Muslims are benefited by the partition and the minority communities on both sides of the border suffer a lot.

Sidhwa's true talent lies in highlighting every aspect of a character with the eternal conflict of moral good and malevolent instinct in the human spirit. The Ice-candy man, Dilnawaz is an ebullient and sociable man. His mother belonged to the prostitute market of Lahore and somewhere Ice-candy man's personality and taste are under the influence of this evil market. He sells ice-candy in summer and becomes a bird seller in winter. The novelist introduces the theme of lust and desire through the character of the Ice-candy man. He is a gifted poet and an ardent lover of the Hindu Ayah. But he becomes a different person the day he witnesses the arrival of the train full of the mutilated bodies of his Muslim brethren from Gurudaspur. Ice Candy-Man's relatives lie dead in the heap of corpses in the ill-fated train. His beloved Ayah becomes a Hindu for him. The Ice-candy man, Dilnawaz's desire is constant but lack of restraint and good sense unleash the beast inside him. He becomes the leader of a fanatic mob and dishonestly betrays his love, "they drag Ayah out. They drag her by her arms stretched taut, and her bare feet that want to move backwards—are forced forward instead." (183).

In contrast of the character of the Ice-candy man, Sidwa sketches the character of Masseur and Imam Din who are the source of love, trust and brotherood in the novel. Masseur has an objective view and is always trying to diffuse the tension with his sensible talking. When the rumors of communal riot breaks out, Masseur, one of the Muslim admirers of Ayah, promises to marry Ayah and protect her. In contrast, Ice-Candy-Man not only abducts the Ayah and throws her to the wolves of passion in the prostitute market but also kills her out of jealousy for his co-religionist Masseur. Besides Masseur there is one more character of Imam Din's whose entire family has been wiped out in Pir Pindo and Ranna alone has survived to tell the gruesome tale. Sidhwa deftly hands over the narration to Lenny, who narrates the story of the changing pattern of communal relations. The description of Ranna's village shows the animalistic characteristic of men where the Sikhs mercilessly kill the Muslims. In the same way, Ice-candy man is also blinded by the religious hatred and revenge turns him into a cruel man who derives atrocious pleasure and satisfaction in killing the Hindus and Sikhs. But Imam Din, a simple cook sets another example of humanity. He remains calm in the face of all calamities and destruction. The distinction between the two characters (Imam Din and Ice-candy man) becomes marked when a mob of fanatic Muslims comes to abduct the Ayah. At that time, Imam Din goes to the extent of telling a lie about Ayah: "Allah-ki-Kasam, she's gone." (182) Thus, the novelist shows that the defenders of Islam who turned Lahore into a burning city were not true advocates of Islam. But Imam Din and Masseur are the real followers of Islam and shine in the novel. The character of Masseur and Imam Din are like an oasis of communal fraternity in the desert of communal hostility.

The novel interprets the plight of the people who became victims of this ghastly incident of Indian history. Chaos, confusion and mayhem become the order of the day.

The chaos and confusion bring out the tragedy of the partition. Like Sidhwa, Lenny plays a role of a detached observer who sees the trauma of partition and separations it involves. She has remained objective in the sense that all have tried to expose human nature and its capability of carrying out cruelty and barbarism on its own creed.The good and bad aspect of the partition are discussed and argued amongst friends and colleagues of the five main communities of Lahore, the Hindus, Muslims, Sikhs, Christians and Parsees. The novelist digs out the fact that all passions whether religious or amorous are capable of bringing out the best and the worst in human beings. Religious hatred led to communal violence. Discussing the fate of Punjab in the event of Partition, Masseur hopes that if Punjab is divided, Lahore will go to Pakistan and in contrast the Government House gardener hopes that this will not come true as the Hindus have much of their money invested there. The discussion of Masseur and the gardener reflects the environment of Lahore. Like Bapsi Sidhwa, Attia Hosain has also focused on the never-ending offensive debates on the merits and de-merits of the partition. Kemal and Saleem, the two real brothers argued on the partition in *Sunlight on a Broken Column*. But there is a difference between the two women novelists. Attia Hosain does not dig deep into the gory details of the butcheries and destruction of the partition. She logically and ethically presents the different aspects of the partition through the rich family of Taluqdars. But Sidhwa depicts the events reaching the Partition in their naked cruelty and heartlessness. However, the end of the novel is similar to *Sunlight on a Broken Column* and both the women novelists stress on the unavoidable logic of the partition which moves on inexorably leading to friends and families being separated and lost from each other. In *Sunlight on a Broken Column,* Attia shows how the two real brothers and lovers are separated because of religious differences and the partition. Laila, the heroine of the novel and Kemal, her cousin lost everything in the partition including family, property and reputation. People of different communities, friends and colleagues argue about the impossibility of violence against each other and leaving their homeland. In the same way, Bapsi Sidhwa also focuses on the families and friends who met every evening at Queens Park in Lahore and are separated forever due to partition. As Novy Kapadiastates:

"Both narrator- heroines, Lenny in Ice Candy Man and Laila in Sunlight on a Broken Column, react against communal responses to the horror of violence. The mature Laila rationalizes against communal tension whereas the young Lenny instinctively reacts against the horror of communal violence." (The Novels of, Kapadia & Dhawan, 41)

Bapsi Sidhwa delicately threads the story of Lenny with the din of violence ready to crash around her world as the Partition moves from political planning into reality. Along with political ineffectiveness, the author depicts the malicious nature of the differences between the Congress and the Muslim League on the ordinary people of India which is rightly anticipated by Sharbat Khan when he cautions Ayah, "These are bad timesAllah knows what's in store. There is big trouble in Calcutta and Delhi: Hindu-Muslim trouble. The Congress-wallahs are after Jinnah's blood." (75) Ayah, however, shakes off this caution with a casual remark, "What's it to us if Jinnah, Nehru and Patel fight? They are not fighting our fight," (75). The remark of the Ayah shows her ignorance towards the political condition of the country. It also symbolises that the common people are not aware of the political conditions during the partition. However, Sharbat Khan does not agree with her assessment and is of the opinion that though that "may be true but they are stirring up trouble for us all." (75-76)

Here he becomes the voice of the novelist and comments that it was the intransigent sectarianism of the national leaders which wrought havoc on the pattern of communal amity existing in rural India.Mr. Singh, however, thinks that once India gains Independence, they will be able to settle all their differences, as these have been created by the British.She introduces the conversations among ordinary people in the novel through which she offers the perspective of the marginalized. The insignificant characters of the novel such as Masseur, the Government House gardener and Sher Singh give a glimpse of the analyst and critic. They analyse and draw their own interpretations which sometimes reflect the stand taken by the respective communal groups to which they belong. But they also curse the politicians in whose hands their destiny lies. The author through common people comments sarcastically on the Indian politicians. The butcher's comment on Gandhi is typical of a Muslim in the pre-Partition context: That non-violent violence mongeryour precious Gandhiji first declares the Sikhs fanatics! Now suddenly he says: "Oh dear, the poor Sikhs cannot live with the Muslims if there is aPakistan!" What does he think we aresome kind of beast? Aren't they living with us now? (91) The Masseur's reply is equally satirical: "He's a politician, yaar. It's his business to suit his tongue to the moment." (91)

Sidhwa comments on Gandhi's personality and presents her view through Lenny, "He is small, dark, shrivelled, old. He looks just like Hari, our gardener, except he has a disgruntled, disgusted and irritable look, and no one'd dare pull off his dhoti! He wears only the loin-dhoti and his black and thin torso is naked". (86) The author unhesitantly pointed out on Gandhi's interest in women, "He is knitting. Sitting cross-legged on the marble floor of a palatial veranda, he is surrounded by women." (86-87) The novelist also uses a humorous tone when she describes his routine, "Gandhiji certainly is ahead of his times. He already knows the advantage of dieting. He has starved his way into the news and made headlines all over the world." (86) She also shows some respect towards some of his deeds, "He is a man who loves women. And lame children. And the untouchable sweeper's constipated girl-child best." (87) Through these remarks, the author wants to touch the nerve of the common people. Reena Mitra opines:

> "The humour is something mistaken ribaldry but in-depth analysis of the novel shows that all the humour, laughter and mirth employed is with a purpose. It is through their ribald humour and rustic wisdom that Ayah as also Lenny's companions enable the little girl to chronicle the tragedy of the partition." (Critical..., Mitra, 114)

Like Chaman Nahal, Bapsi Sidhwa also goes through the political aspect of the partition. This issue has become the keynote of her narrative. Like Nahal, she also re-evaluates the role of the British and their policy of divide and rule during their rule which leads the subcontinent on the path of the partition. She considers the partition a tragedy and mistake of the leaders which could have been avoided. Sidhwa likes to call her a Pakistani and her sensitiveness towards her country is truly highlighted in the novel. Unlike Attia Hosain, she claims how Partition has favoured India over Pakistan. She totally discards the perspectives of the Indian novelists and historians. She attempts to expose the part of the Indian leaders and the British over Jinnah. She contends:

> "For now, the tide is turned- and the Hindus are being favoured over the Muslims by the remnants of the Raj. Now that its objective to divideIndiais achieved, the British favour Nehru over Jinnah. Nehru is Kashmiri, they grant him Kashmir. Spurning logic, defying rationale, ignoring the consequence of bequeathing a Muslim state to the Hindus. . . They grant Nehru Gurdaspur and Pathankot without which Kashmir cannot be secured." (159)

Sidhwa presents herself as a Pakistani writer and that essence of her personality reflects in her work. The background and the Muslim culture are noticeable in the novel. She overthrows the prevalent tale about the Partition which has fostered in the countries, India and Pakistan. Unlike Nahal, she defends Jinnah and does not consider him as the reason of the partition. Through Lenny she expresses her own thought:

> "But didn't Jinnah, too, die of a broken heart? And today, forty years later, in films of Gandhi's and Mountbatten's lives, in books by British and Indian scholars, Jinnah, who for a decade was

known as 'Ambassador of Hindu-Muslim Unity',
is caricatured, and portrayed as a monster." (160)

She shows the popular image of Jinnah with the help of an ordinary sepoy, "don't underestimate Jinnah,' says the off-duty sepoy. 'He will stick within his rights, no matter whom Nehru feeds! He's a first-rate lawyer and he knows how to attack the British with their own laws!'" (131) Sidhwa also talks about Jinnah's wife who was a Parsi and amazingly beautiful, "large eyes, liquid-brown, radiating youth, promising intelligence, declaring innocence, shining from an oval marble-firm face. Full-lipped, delighting in the knowledge of her own loveliness..." (160) Unlike Bapsi Sidhwa, Chaman Nahal criticises Jinnah for spreading misleading information regarding the Hindus and Sikhs. He blames Jinnah and the Muslim league for inflaming hatred among simple people to serve their own selfish ends. The Muslims were manipulated and involved in violence by Jinnah's call of direct action during the partition. Jinnah highlighted small problems among the parties to make it a big issue for his own benefit and pushed the country towards the partition.

Bapsi Sidhwa's Ice-Candy-Man constantly works on historical facts to stress on the important and notable features of the politics during the partition. The crippling attack of the partition kept the subcontinent in the throes of the disaster and in chaos. The main focus of the novelist is to highlight the partition of the subcontinent and the politics surrounding and responsible for it that eventually resulted in innumerable tragedies, and disaster for both the countries. The novelist presents the views and perspectives of her nation by focusing on the political conspiracies of Mountbatten, Nehru and Patel to cripple Pakistan by depriving it of its rightful resources, "Jinnah or no Jinnah! Sikh or no Sikh! Right law, wrong law, Nehru will walk off with the lions share…" (131) Randhir Pratap Singh comments:

> "Most of the political heavyweights of the time – Gandhi, Nehru, Jinnah, Iqbal, Patel, Bose, Master Tara Singh, Lord Mountbattenfigure in Ice-Candy-Man in some context or the other but whereas the Hindus leaders have been presented in an unfavourable maner, the portrayal of Jinnah evokes admiration and sympathy." (Bapsi Sidhwa, Singh, 55)

Sidhwa raises questions on Nehru's loyalty by exposing his relations with Lady Mountbatten; "He bandies words with Lady Mountbatten and is presumed to be her lover. He is charming, too, to Lord Mountbatten." (159) Nehru is bitterly criticised by common people, "But that Nehru, he's a sly one… He's got Mountbatten eating out of his one hand and the English's wife out of his other what-out…. He's one to watch." (131) The comments of the common people like butcher and Masseur show that the communal frenzy and the feeling of abhorrence is so intense that people are unaware of Mahatma Gandhi and Nehru's contribution and sacrifices in the freedom struggle. But their observations and their clarifications on the latest political developments provide the chance to readers to understand the communal and political condition of the subcontinent during the partition. Reena Mitra speaks out:

> "Bapsi Sidhwa's ICM warrants the careful critical attention of those interested in new possibilities for imaginative prose which resorts to viable fictional

meanslargely realisticfor tracing the pressure of history on individual lives, presenting a collage of the lives and experience of men and women caught in the web of history." (Critical..., Mitra, 24)

The novelist introduces the concept of manipulation and betrayal through the different characters of the novel. The character of the Ice-Candy man represents the manipulative and unsympathetic nature. His character also reflects lust and desire throughout the novel. His selfishness is shown by the fact that he keeps his wife in the village and he wants to possess the Ayah even after being married. He plays the role of a pimp in the novel and his manipulative nature forces him to betray the Ayah, who has trusted him. The Ayah is not only betrayed by Ice-candy man but also her other friends. Even Lenny is a part of this betrayal but the novelist presents her to be innocent because Lenny betrays the Ayah unintentionally. With another example of Godmother, on the one hand, the author portrays the character of the Godmother as the source of strength but on the other side she manipulates and suppresses the Slave sister and sometimes she has misused her power. The aim of the novelist to show this relationship is to focus on the fact that manipulation and exploitation are not restricted to only men but also women. Bapsi Sidhwa explores the theme of disloyalty and unfaithfulness during the partition. She exposes the misuse of power by the leaders who have born the responsibility of the subcontinent during and after the partition. The power-hungry politicians do not care about the common and innocent people who have no idea about the partition. The novel reflects the unemotional and impassive nature of the British government.

Ice-Candy-Manis a postcolonial novel in which the novelist presents thehistory ofthe subcontinent from the perspective of a young girl, Lenny. The novelist very skilfully describes the horror of the Partition with the complications of life after Independence. Her fiction not only brings to life the gory events but reaches the aim of dismantling philosophies of spirit and genuineness. The novelist intensely portrays the political and social condition of the subcontinent before and after the partition. As Alamgir Hashmi observes:

> "The new post-colonial modes have also arisen from new philosophical and literary interests... two of Bapsi Sidhwa's three novels, 'The Crow Eaters' and Ice-Candy-Man, have, on another plane of performance, introduced a farcical strain to the Pakistani novel in English, a strain in which "sacred facts" appear laughable, and family and communal reservations and loyalties are put to a serve comic or eccentric test, even if it is only to explain, rationalize or accept those very facts."
> (Major Minorities, Granqvist, 108)

InIce-Candy-Man, Sidhwa grapples with the realities of the pre and post-Independence period. The most notable and significant fact about her work is her dual perspective. Her novel is based on both the Pakistani and the Parsi point of view. Her writing captures the sense of tragedy and trauma of the turbulent times of partition of India in 1947. The author uses the tone of the gloomy sense of humour to describe the traumatic event of human history.Bapsi Sidhwa reveals how the violence of partition has jagged the roots of people of different communities, inspite of ideology, friendship and rational beliefs. Attia Hosain and Bapsi Sidhwa both female writers try to expose the partition as the most tragic event of Indian history. It is a bold and successful attempt from the women writers to take up a theme which is different from the traditional issues. The novelist adopts an optimistic approach towards the end of the novel. Like Attia Hosain and Chaman Nahal, Bapsi Sidhwa also gives a positive message that one should start a new life after going through adversity. All the three novelists have advocated a new start. Laila in *Sunlight on a Broken Column* starts a new life after leaving her past life and the memories of her husband behind. In the same way, Lala Kanshi Ram begins his new life after losing everything in the partition including his daughter. Bapsi Sidhwa also presents the same concept through Parsi women who work towards the healing process for the fallen women who are abandoned for no fault of their own. Even Ice candy man has taken a step on the path of moral good when he understands that he will not get the Ayah's love. Attia Hosain's protagonist, Laila feels, "....I was my own prisoner and could release myself."(*Sunlight*, Attia Hosain, 319) She means that now she is ready to start her life with a fresh approach after leaving all the painful memories behind. Besides this, Attia also presents an ideal example of Hindu Muslim reconciliation through the character of Saleem, cousin of Laila. After the partition, Saleem leaves India for Pakistan but after two years when he comes back to India, he is shocked to see the healthy environment between the two communities and says, "I am glad you are effete enough to forget your political affiliations, to say, 'Welcome, friend' and not 'Go back traitor!" (*Sunlight..*, Attia Hosain, 301)

In the same way, when Ice-candy man leaves Lahore for Amritsar, he sets an example of self-sacrifice. Through this Sidhwa gives the symbolic message of the future reunion between the two belligerent communities, the Hindus and the Muslims. Even Chaman Nahal also leaves the same message when Lala Kanshi Ram says, "I have ceased to hate... I can't hate the Muslims anymore."(*Azadi*, Nahal, 298)

These are the examples, through which one can understand the positive approach of the novelists. They are endeavouring to locate such symbolic incidents in the novel. In other words, all the three novelists point out that the only way to heal wounds is to face them with determination and to overcome them by forgiving and helping others who have gone through the worst.

Works Cited

Book Review of R. K. Narayan's The World of Nagraj, Sunday, 11-17 Nov, 1990.

Didur, Jill. "Cracking the Nation: Memory, Minorities and the Ends of Narrative in Bapsi Sidhwa's *Cracking India*", *Unsettling Partition: Literature, Gender, Memory,* New Delhi: University of Toronto,2006, 93

Engineer, Asghar Ali.*Communalism in India: A Historical and Empirical Study*, New Delhi: Vikas Publishing House, 1995, 28.

Gopal, Priyamvada. "Writing Partition" *The Indian English Novel: Nation, History and Narration* New York :Oxford University Press, 2009, 75

Hashmi, Alamgir "Prolegomena to the study of Pakistani English and Pakistani Literature in English" Major Minorities English Literature in Transit ed. Raoul Granqvist Amsterdam: Atlanta, GA, 1993, 108

Hosain, Attia. *Sunlight on a Broken Column* New Delhi: Penguin Group, 1961, 319

Kanaganayakam, Chelva. "Allegory and Ambivalence in Bapsi Sidhwa's Cracking India," *Parsi Fiction*, Vol.2, Ed. Novy Kapadia, Jaydiosinh Dodiya and R. K. Dhawan New Delhi: Prestige, 2000,43

Kapadia, Novy. "Communal Frenzy and Partition: Bapsi Sidhwa, Attia Hosain and Amitav Ghosh", *The Novels of Bapsi Sidhwa* Ed. R.K.Dhawan & Novy Kapadia, New Delhi: Prestige, 1996, 41.

Mitra, Reena. "Bapsi Sidhwa's Ice Candy Man: A Reassessment" *Critical Response to Literature in English* New Delhi: Atlantic Publishers & Distributers, 2005, 114

Nahal,Chaman. *Azadi* New Delhi: orient Paperback, 1975, 110

Nimsarkar, P. D. "Dimensionality of History and Politics in Bapsi Sidhwa's Ice Candy Man" *Contemporary Fiction: An Anthology of Female Writers* Ed. Urmila Dabir New Delhi: Sarup & Sons, 2008, 78.

Ray, Sangeeta. "New Women, New Nations: Writing the partition in Desai's clear Light of Day and Sidhwa's Cracking India" *En-Gendering India: Woman and Nation in Colonial and Postcolonial Narratives* USA: Duke University Press, 2000, 137

Sidhwa, Bapsi. "Ice-Candy-Man" New Delhi: Penguin Group, 1988, 180. (All the subsequent references given in the parenthesis are from this edition)

Singh, Randhir Pratap "Partition Revisited" Bapsi Sidhwa New Delhi: IVY publishing house, 2005, 55

CONCLUSION

The partition of the Indian sub-continent in 1947 orchestrated by the British led to one of the ghastly orgies of violence the world has ever seen, the magnitude of which is apparent even today. Religious fanaticism brutally squashed the unique ideal of non-violence shattering the dream of united and secular India as people started wallowing in bonds of communal mayhem. A mania for murder swept across northern India and Pakistan for six terrible long weeks. The Muslims on the one hand, and the Sikhs and the Hindus on the other callously butchered one another. The purge that occurred over quarters of a million people were done to death and several lakhs of people rendered homeless. Communal frenzy caused huge exodus of population on both the sides. People in the street wept with sorrow when the partition was announced. It is the country's tortured past. The partition has left a legacy of hatred between the people of two new dominions.

The four novels selected provide insightful information about the critical and harrowing event of the partition. The selection of the novels depends upon their being works with a major thrust on the partition. The time period covered by the novelists is from 1961 to 1988. This also reflects the changes if any, in the approach of the novelists and also the changes which can be noticed by the fact that the novelists belong to different parts of the sub-continent. Despite these differences, there is much that they share. They are the authors of the partition narratives and their narrative represents the events leading up to the Partition and as well as the immediate aftermath of the partition of India. In their choice of subject matter and narrative form, all of them respond to the partition as a traumatic event. The consequences of the partition have been explored by the authors of the partition narratives. They dig into the relationship between gender, memory, and trauma of the partition with the help of the setting of the novel as an art form. As the theme of the research work is partition, the four novelists who are the object of study, offer us an opportunity to analyse the various perspectives of the partition from different angles. These novels are based on the insane butcheries committed in the name of religion before and after the partition. The overlapping of history and fiction is also exhibited in these novels. The novelists have claimed that the ill treatment meted out to the masses during the partition resulted in emotional and psychological distress. Partition novels somewhere deal with the communal problem of India. As India was set to achieve freedom, communalists prepared to take benefit from the differences among all the parties and creeds. There were members of national parties who supported the Congress and at the same time the Hindu Mahasabha or the Muslim League. Thus, they were directly responsible for the disaster.

The novelists have described the event in their novels as eye - witnesses to the holocaust of the Partition. Instead of criticising the partition, some novelists prefer to present the agony, loss and destruction caused by the partition. Since 1956, after Khushwant Singh there has been a continuous stream of writing about this event. The emotional separation caused by the partition is one of the most unfortunate events in the history of mankind. However, the trauma cannot be assessed by the politicians, historians or the religious leaders but great novelists like Khushwant Singh, Malgaonkar, Chaman Nahal, Attia Hosain etc. have been able to depict the magnanimous tragedy of human values in their fictional work. Although Mulk Raj Anand, R.K. Narayan and Raja Rao depicted the freedom struggle and the impact of Gandhi's ideology in their novels, they did not deal directly with the Partition in their writings as did Khushwant Singh or Chaman Nahal. The theme of the partition has not been treated only in English fiction but also in other regional languages of India like Hindi, Marathi, Sindhi, Punjabi, Bengali, Urdu and even more. There are many novelists who dealt with the subject but Ramanand Sagar was the ground breaker in the field. His novel *Aur Insaan Mar Gaya* published in 1948, is the first novel on the partition of India. This novel was translated under the title *Bleeding Partition* and published in 1984. The novel has four volumes with distinct characters of both communities. It was translated into Marathi under the title *Aani Manasacha Mudada Padala* by Shripad Joshi in 1963. Beside this, there are also some other Hindi novels like Yashpal's *Jhoota Sach,* Nasim Hijazi's *Khaak aur Khoon*, Rahi Masoom Raza's Aadha Gaon, Krishna Baldev Vaid's The Broken Mirror (a Hindi novel), Kamleshwar's Kitne Pakistan and Laute Huye Musafir. Some Urdu novelists have also expressed their rage, fear and anxiety towards the partition. The prominent among them is Saadat Hasan Manto who remonstrates against the partition and appeals for communal harmony in his novel Toba Tek Singh. Intizar Hussain's Basti, Mumtaz Mufti's Ali *Pur Ka Aeeli*, Abdulla Hussain's *The Weary Generations,* K. M. Abbas's *Mai Kaun hun* and several other novels depict the pathetic event.

The fictional narratives of Pakistan also articulate these inhuman experiences of the tumultuous period that immediately followed independence. Mumtaz Shah Nawaz, a Pakistani woman writer and a political activist, had responded to the colonial experience and the Partition in her novel. *The Heart Divided* which was published after her death in 1957 was the first novel on the partition of India, in English literature.It was Nawaz' first and last novel as she was killed in an air crash over Ireland in 1948. She was 35. *The Heart Divided* traces the factors and the circumstances which headed to the Partition of the sub-continent and the formation of Pakistan. The story is partly autobiographical. It is almost a documentary account of the life of children in a well-to-do Muslim family in Lahore in the '30s. The title of the novel reflects towards "the manifold complexities of dividing the 'nation' which is assumed, in the first instance, to be an organic whole but is, in fact, a complex construct with its own contradictions." (Indian Eng. Novel, Gopal, 74)

The novel has the assorted themes surrounding the Partition and the impression of colonization upon indigenous ethos. Krishna Kumar rightly commented,

> "The novel shows that historian make a serious mistake when they seek the reasons for Partition in the familiar triangle of the Congress, the Muslim League and the British. The story brings out the partition that had already occurred by the late

1930s in the heart, that is to say, in the universe of emotions and personal relations.... In its early spring, it presented to the Hindu and Muslim elites an impossible demandto mix more deeply or to separate." (*Battle...*, Kumar, 81)

The theme of the novel has spontaneity and the main characters are clearly delineated in the book. Habib falls in love with a Kashmiri Brahmin girl and wants to marry her in the hope that their marriage would set an example for a free and united India. The character of Habib and his sister, Zohra shows inclination towards the unity between the Muslim League and the Congress. Later, they blame the latter for the partition. Mumtaz left a ray of hope for the reunion of both the communities as well as both the countries through her novel. Shah Nawaz was fretful for the rights of the women which she highlights in her novel also.

Kamila Shamsie, the author of Salt and Saffron, is great-niece of Attia Hosain. She was born in 1973 and brought up in Pakistan. Kamila Shamsie is one of a new waves of Pakistani writers who are settled in Britain and successful in both Pakistan and the West. The theme of her novel also centres around partition and freedom struggle. Her protagonist, Aliya belongs to an aristocratic family like Laila in *Sunlight on a broken Column* by Attia Hosain. The character of Laila can be compared with the character of Aliya in Salt and Saffron. The similarity between the two novels is that both the novelists belong to the same family. Aliyareacquaints with her family members after being away for four years at a university in America. She meets her relatives first in London and then in Karachi. After meeting her relatives, she becomes aware of those aspects of her family's story which she never knew, especially those related to the Partition of India which also divided the family. The backgrounds of both the novels are set in a high rank Muslim family and both aristocratic families disintegrated because of the partition. Salt and Saffron directly deals with shock and pain of the partition and disturbances in family relations which affects generations. As Jopi Nyman observed,

> "Since partition can be discussed as a major national trauma in both Indian and Pakistani culture, its literary representations appear to rework its legacy.... The notion of partition is the central metaphor of the novel, and it can be found at various levels extending from—and linking—the political to the personal....the novel is not a mere narrative of contemporary diasporic communities, but it develops such thematics by exploring aspects of (in)voluntary exile, migration, and separation. In so doing, it shows their traumatizing effects for families and individuals." (Home Identity, Jopi, 110-112)

The protagonist of both the novels struggle for the freedom and try to control their life. But Aliya, the daughter of urban, Karachi professional does not show any bitterness for the partition like Laila but she is worried and preoccupied by the harsh argument between her Pakistani grandparents and their Indian relatives. Although, belonging to the same family, they are different in their perspectives. Both the novelists reflect their period of time and the time space between the two generations. As S. R. Chakravarty and Mazhar Hussain rightly notes,

"The Indian subcontinent has been partitioned into three independent states, but the literature and culture are yet to be divided. Iqbal, Rabindranath, Nazrul etc., have not been divided.... Creative art and literature of the day, be they Indian, Pakistani or Bangladeshi, are still strengthening the age old composite and syncretic culture of the sub-continent... The idea of a state based on a particular religion and the movement for it has not by and large appeal to artists and writers." (Partition...literary responses, Chakravarty & Hussain, 28)

All the novelists make it clear that people belonging to the sub-continent were conscious of the superfluous differences among them. They were completely forgetful of the fact that they had common ancestors, history and heritage. Though the novelists have had their views and opinions, one thing which is established in the passage of time, is that the overall impact of the partition has been very disastrous to both the countries India and Pakistan. The geographical partition of the subcontinent produced the historic antagonisms between the two countries. The Partition undesirably and poorly affected the life of common man on both sides of the border as well. Ever since India has been suffering from the disastrous events like the Bombay blast and attack on the parliament to name a few. At the time of independence, India and Pakistan had faced the civil turbulence as well as ethnic and religious discord which threatened the stability and the peace of both the countries. During the partition, major tensions have persisted between the Muslim and Sikh communities. Both the communities had suffered most from the violence and land loss as a result of the partition. The religious clashes led to a trench between the Hindus and the Muslims which have hindered the effective functioning of civil administration. The destruction of the Muslim shrine at Ayodhya in 1992 was an example of this, in which both the communities were equally affected. But India has maintained a remarkable level of cohesion since independence. Indian politicians had ratified a constitution, which led to the first democratic elections in 1951. This has made India the world's largest democracy and consolidated governmental authority over the entire subcontinent.

The event of the partition is the consequence of the British politics, and conflict between Communalism and Nationalism of the Hindus and Muslims. The Partition of the subcontinent created political and domestic problems for both the countries and posed a threat to the South Asian identity. In the thirty years of independence, India and Pakistan fought three wars, two over Kashmir, and one over the creation of an independent Bangladesh. It has given birth to the most important Kashmir problem which has been an apple of discord since 1947. After the death of Mohammed Ali Jinnah in 1948, the conflict over the Princely State of Kashmir, to which both the countries have claimed their right was commenced. The fate of Kashmir was left undetermined at the time when the British left India. Kashmir was claimed by both countries, which have been at war in 1965, 1971 and the Kargil incident which were initiated by Pakistan, though India has always been on the defensive. The war has wasted thousands of lives and millions of dollars. On the other hand, Pakistan is suffering under the agonizing tyranny of military rule. The ethnic and religious differences within Pakistan prevented and impeded the early attempts to agree on a constitution and successful working of a government. From the point of view of the Muslims, the severe blow of the partition was felt not only by the Muslims who left India, but also by those who chose to stay back in India. They endured the suspicious and angry attitude of the Hindus. The outcome of the partition was that the Muslims were discriminated in every field such as employment or business. The most tragic part of the partition was faced by the younger generations who were not even in the world at the time of the partition. These are the gifts of the partition which play with the life of innocent people. The holocaust, trauma, betrayal, tragedy, mass displacement, communal riots, huge loss of lives and property, atrocities and violent inhuman acts are the ironic rewards of the partition which have made life hell for both the countries. It has left an everlasting blemish on the soul of the victims.

Partition was not acceptable to anyone, neither the Hindus nor the Muslims. Both the communities suffered during and after the partition. The purpose of partition has been defeated. The British have left the country but their policy of 'divide and rule' still persists. Now politicians are doing it for their own vested interests. The Partition was headed and directed by the extensive coverage of butchery, rape, terror, trepidation, arson, rebellion hostility, distrust, religious enmity, attacks and counter-attacks. However, human values were still there amid all the savagery, butchery and mayhem. The few rare people who valued and maintained humanitarianism were the ray of hope, the stalwarts of society who became saviours for the suffering and oppressed masses. These people are like shafts of light which spread faith and optimism with the hope that the restoration of humanism and propagation of communal harmony would be established between the two communities. Even literature relating to the partition mirrors the communal narrow mindedness and religious fanaticism but it also echoes the human values which are well-maintained by individuals in both the warring communities even in the midst of utter turmoil.

Instead of solving any problem faced by the common people, the partition of India produced many of them that remain unsettled even today. Today both the countries are trying to establish a healthy relationship not only with each other but also among the communities, the Hindu, Muslim and Sikh. If achieved, it might finally achieve the dreams of Mahatma Gandhi and once more set an example for post-colonial societies. Attia Hosain rightly remarked, "all accounts and history have proved that 'yes', there is a logic in history that the fight for unity should have won against all odds, not the fight for disunity." (Interview of Attia)

Works Cited

Chakravarty, S. R. and Hussain, Mazhar (Ed), 'Introduction' *Partition of India: Literary Responses,* New Delhi: Har-Anand Publications, 1988.

Gopal, Priyamvada. "Writing Partition" *The Indian English Novel: Nation, History and Narration*, New York: Oxford University Press, 2009.

Hosain, Attia. Interview by Omar Khan, Harappa.com. London, 19 May 1991.

Kumar, Krishna. *Battle for peace,* New Delhi: Penguin Books, 2007, 81.

Nyman, Jopi. *Home, Identity and Mobility in Contemporary Diasporic Fiction,* New York: Rodopi, 2009.

BIBLIOGRAPHY

Primary Sources:

Hosain, Attia. *Sunlight on a Broken Column*. New Delhi: Penguin Group, 1961.

Malgaonkar, Manohar. *A Bend in the Ganges*. New Delhi: Saurabh Printers, 1964.

Nahal, Chaman. *Azadi*. New Delhi: Orient Paperback, 1975.

Sidhwa, Bapsi. *Ice Candy Man*. New Delhi: Penguin Group, 1988.

Secondary Sources:

Agarwal, K.A. *Indian Writing in English: A Critical Study*. New Delhi: Atlantic Publishers, 2003.

Anjaneyulu, T.A. *Critical Study of the Selected Novels of Mulk Raj Anand, Manohar Malgaonkar and Khushwant Singh*. New Delhi: Atlantic Publishers, 1998.

Amur, G.S. *Manohar Malgaonkar*. New Delhi: Arnold Heinemann, 1973.

Asnani, Shyam. *Critical Response to Indian English Fiction*. New Delhi: Mittal, 1985.

Awasthi, Kamal N. *Contemporary Indian English Fiction: An Anthology of Essays*. Jalander: ABS Publication, 1998.

Bhatta, S.C. *The Literary Criterion, Vol. XII, Nos. 2-3*, 1976, 228

Booker, M. Keith. *Colonial Power, Colonial Texts: India in the Modern British Novel.* USA: University of Michigan Press, 1997.

Bolitho, Hector. *Jinnah: Creator of Pakistan*, London: John Murray, 1954.

Burton, Antoinette. *Dwelling in the Archive: Women Writing House, Home, and History in Late Colonial India.* New York: Oxford University Press, 2003.

Chakravarty, Joya (Ed). *Indian writing in English: perspectives.* New Delhi: Atlantic Publishers and Distributers, 2003.

Chakravarty, S. R. and Hussain, Mazhar. *Partition of India: Literary Responses,* New Delhi: Har-Anand Publications, 1998.

Chandra, Bipin. *Communalism in Modern India.* New Delhi: Har Anand Publication, 1984.

Chandra, N.D.R. *Modern Indian Writing in English: Critical Perceptions.* Vol.1 New Delhi: Sarup & Sons, 2004.

Collins, Larry & Dominique. *Lapierre Mountbatten and the partition of India.* New Delhi: Vikas Publishing House, 1984.

Dabir, Urmila. *Contemporary Fiction: An Anthology of Female Writers.* New Delhi: Sarup & Sons, 2008.

Das, Manmath Nath. *Partition and Independence of India.* New Delhi: Vision Books, 1982.

Desai, Anita. Introduction, Sunlight on a Broken Column by Attia Hosain, New Delhi: Penguin Group, 1961.

Dhawan, R.K. & Kapadia, Novy. *The Novels of Bapsi Sidhwa*. New Delhi: Prestige, 1996.

Dhawan, R.K. *Exploration in Modern Indo-English Fiction*. New Delhi: Bahri Publication, 1982.

----- Ed. *Three Contemporary Novelists*. New Delhi: Classical Publishing Company, 1985.

---- Ed. *Modern Indo-English Fiction*. New Delhi: Bahri Publication, 1982.

---- Ed. *Commonwealth Fiction*. Vol. I. New Delhi: Classical Publishing Company, 1988.

Didur, Jill. *Unsettling Partition: Literature, Gender, Memory*. New Delhi: University of Toronto, 2006.

Dwievedi, A.N. (Ed). *Studies in Contemporary Indian Fiction in English*. Allahabad: Kitab Mahal, 1987.

Engineer, Asghar Ali. *Communalism in India: A Historical and Empirical Study*, New Delhi: Vikas Publishing House, 1995.

Fleishman, Avrom. *The English Historical Novel: Walter Scott to Virginia Woolf*. London: The Johns Hopkins Press, 1971.

Gill, H.S. *Ashes and Petals*. New Delhi: Vikas Publication, 1978.

Gill, Raj. *The Rape*. New Delhi: Vikas Publication, 1974.

Gopal, Priyamvada. *The Indian English Novel: Nation, History and Narration*, New York: Oxford University Press, 2009.

Granqvist, Raoul. *Major Minorities English Literature in Transit.* Amsterdam: Atlanta, GA, 1993.

Hays, Merrian Allen (Ed). **Gandhi Vs Jinnah: The Debate Over the Partition. Calcutta: Minerva Associates, 1980.**

Heehs, Peter. *India's Freedom Struggle (1857-1947).* Delhi: Oxford University Press, 1988.

Hasan, Mushirul. *Nationalism and Communal Politics in India 1885-1930.* Delhi: **Manohar Publishers and Distributors, 1994.**

Hudson, W.H. *An Introduction to the Study of Literature,* 7th edision. Ludhiana: Kalyani Publishers, 1976.

Iyer, N. Sharda. *Musing on Indian Writing in English: Fiction.* New Delhi: Sarup & Sons, 2003.

Iyengar, K.R. Srinivasa. *Indian Writing in English in Contemporary Indian Literature,* 2nd edition. New Delhi: Sahitya Akademi, 1959.

---- Ed. *Indian Writing in English, Bombay: Asia Publishing House, 1962.*

Jain, Jasbir & Amina Amin. *Margins of Erasure.* New Delhi: Sterling Publisher, 1995.

Jalal, Ayesha (Ed). ***The Sole Spokesman: Jinnah, the Muslim League and the Demand for Pakistan* (paperback Ed.). Cambridge: Cambridge University Press, 1994.**

Juneja, Om P. *Post Colonial Novels.* New Delhi: Creative Books, 1995.

Kapadia, Novy. Dodiya, Jaydiosinh & Dhawan R. K. *Parsi Fiction*, Vol.2, New Delhi: Prestige, 2000.

Kapoor, Manju. *Difficult Daughters*. Delhi: Penguin, 1998.

King, Bruce. *The Internationalization of English Literature* New York: Oxford University Press, 2004.

Kumar, Gajendra. *Indian English Literature: A Post-Colonial Response.* New Delhi: Sarup & Sons, 2005.

Kumar, Krishna. *Battle for peace.* New Delhi: Penguin Books, 2007.

Lapping, Brian, *End of Empire.* London: Granada Publishing, 1985.

Low, D.A. and Howard Brasted. Eds. *Freedom, Trauma, Continuities: Northern India and Independence.* New Delhi: Sage Publications India, 1998.

Mathur, O.P. *Modern English Fiction.* New Delhi: Abhinav Publication, 1993.

Maslen, Elizabeth. *Political, and Social Issues in British Women's Fiction (1928-1968).* New York: Palgrave Macmillan, 2001.

Mehrotra, S.R. *Towards India's Freedom and Partition.* New Delhi: Vikas Publishing House, 1979.

More, D.R. *India & Pakistan: Fell Apart.* Jaipur: Shruti Publication, 2004.

Mukherjee, Meenakshi. *The Twice Born Fiction.* New Delhi: Arnold: 1971.

Mukherjee, Sujit. *Towards a Literary History of India.* Shimla: Indian Institute of Advanced Study, 1975.

Mitra, Reena. *Critical Response to Literature in English.* New Delhi: Atlantic Publishers & Distributors, 2005.

Naik, M. K. *A History of Indian English Literature.* New Delhi: Sahitya Akademi, 1982.

--- *Perspectives on Indian Fiction in English.* New Delhi: Abhinav Publication, 1985.

Naikar, Basavaraj. *Indian English literature Vol.6.* New Delhi: Atlantic publishers & Distributers, 2007.

Needham, Anuradha Dingwaney. *Modern Fiction Studies* 39: 1, 1993.

Nyman, Jopi. *Home, Identity and Mobility in Contemporary Diasporic Fiction,* New York: Rodopi, 2009.

Pandey, Mithilesh K. *Akademi awarded novels in English: Millennium Responses.* New Delhi: Sarup & Sons, 2003.

Prasad, Madhusudan. *Indian English Novelists.* New Delhi: Sterling Publishers Pvt. Ltd., 1982.

Pultar, Gonul. *On the Road to Baghdad or Travelling Biculturalism: Theorizing a Bicultural Approach to Contemporary World Fiction.* USA: New Academia Publishing, 2005.

Rajgopalachari, M. *The Novels of Manohar Malgaonkar.* Delhi: Prestige Books, 1989.

Rao, Pala Prasada, (Ed). *India Pakistan: Partition Perspectives in Indo-English Novels.* New Delhi: Discovering Publishing House, 2004.

Ray, Mohit Kumar & Kundu, Rama. *Salman Rushdie: Critical Essays, Volume*1 New Delhi: Atlantic publication, 2006.

Ray, Sangeeta. *En-Gendering India: Woman and Nation in Colonial and Postcolonial Narratives.* USA: Duke University Press, 2000.

Saini, Rupinderjit "From Harmony to Holocaust: A Study of Community Relations in the Partition Novel", in Journal of the Inter-University Centre for Humanities and Social Sciences Shimla: Rashtrapati Niwas, Nov. 1994, 109

Saint, Tarun K. *Witnessing Partition Memory, History, Fiction.* New Delhi: Routledge, 2010.

Sree, Sathupati Prasanna. *Indian Women Writing in English: New Perspectives* New Delhi: Sarup & Sons, 2005.

Sharma, Ambuj Kumar. *Gandhian Strain in the Indian English Novel.* New Delhi: Sarup & Sons, 2004.

Sharma, K. K. and Johri, B. K. *The Partition in Indo-English Novels* Ghaziabad: Vimal Prakashan, 1984.

Sharma, G.P. *Nationalism in Indo-Anglian Fiction. 1978.* New Delhi: Sterling Publicatins, 1990.

Singh, Randhir Pratap. *Bapsi Sidhwa.* **New Delhi: IVY publishing house, 2005.**

Singh, R.A. and V. Narendra Kumar. Eds. *Critical Studies on Indian Fiction in English.* **New Delhi: Atlantic Publication, 1999.**

Singh, Jaswant(Ed). *Jinnah: India-Partition-Independence.* Oxford: Oxford University Press, 2009.

Walder, Dennis. *Post-Colonial Literature in English: History, Language, Theory.* Oxford, U.K.: Blackwell Publishers, 1998.

William, H.M. *Indo-Anglian Literature* 1800-1970: *A Survey.* New Delhi: Orient Longman, 1976.

William, Walsh. *Indian Literature in English.* London: Longman, 1977.

Book Reviews and Interviews:

Book Review of R. K. Narayan's The World of Nagraj, Sunday, 11-17 Nov, 1990.

Rama Jha, review of Azadi, in Indian Literature, Vol. XXI/5, 1978, 114

Attia Hosain, Interview by Omar Khan, Harappa.com London. 19 may, 1991.

Electronic Media:

http//en.wikipedia.org/wiki/Muhammad_Ali_Jinnaah

www.historytoday.com/ian-talbot/jinnah-and-making-pakistan

www.sikhtimes.com/news-061605a,html-12k

http://www.lehigh.edu/amsp/2006/08/khushwant-singh-journalism.html

http://www.sikh-history.com/sikhist/personalities/ssobha.html

Photographs:

www.punjab partition.com

SUMMARY

In the thesis entitled *A Study of the Theme of the Partition in the Relevant Novels of Attia Hosain, Manohar Malgaonkar, Chaman Nahal, and Bapsi Sidhwa,* an attempt has been made to explore the theme of the partition in the novels of these novelists. The partition of India and Pakistan is indeed the most calamitous event in the history of India. Millions of people died in the riots and children were lost and rendered homeless. Women were kidnapped, raped, and mutilated. The fields were destroyed or left to rot. The dreadful event of the partition led to the world's largest mass exodus which resulted in the separation of families, violence, and callous butchery of innocent people. The division of the subcontinent killed the healthy relations of the Hindus and Muslims who had been living happily for centuries.

The topic 'partition' covers the wealth and treasure of writing in fiction. The history of the partition provides only political facts but the fiction writers have taken the responsibility to highlight the harrowing and painful experiences of people. The enormous loss of human lives and property is felt even after sixty-seven years of the dreadful event. The Hindus, Muslims, and Sikhs fought together against the British in the freedom struggle and later turned enemies of each other.

The format of my thesis contains seven chapters. Chapter I, *Introduction,* studies how political and social changes formed the background of the partition of the subcontinent. The chapter chronicles modern Indian history. The study of the chapter reveals the reasons and circumstances which culminated in the partition. Besides this, some facts from the Muslim historians who present the history of the partition from their perspectives have also been included.

The second chapter, *A Historical Perspective of the Theme of the Partition in Indo-Anglian Novels*, deals with the Indo-Anglian novelists who were affected by the division of the country and have delineated the theme of the partition from their own perspectives. These novelists though living in different parts of the world have been obsessed with the memories of the partition. The novels based on the theme of the partition are weighted down with the misery of mass migration, violence inhuman behaviour, and people rendered nomads. An attempt to analyse the approach of the novelists which portrays the picture of trauma and turbulence including the political condition prevailing during the partition shall also be made. Besides it, there is an attempt to discuss some major novels on the theme of the partition. These novels present the various and different perspectives of the novelists. The theme of the partition has been treated with a purpose in these novels and conveys a moral message of humanity and love.

Chapter III Attia Hosain's *Sunlight on a Broken Column,* deals with the theme of the partition from an Indian Muslim woman's point of view. For Hosain, the novel is nostalgic. Hosain highlights the matters that were ignored in the writings of the partition. She depicts the British as the main cause of the rift between the Hindus and the Muslims. She presents the gradual changes happening in society as well as in the home. Besides, she has also thrown light on the different perspectives of the national Muslims and communal Muslims. Attia introduces the readers to the feudal system which prevailed during British rule and highlights her views against the feudal system through her protagonist Laila. With the help of the character Laila, Hosain tries to unveil the truth of every relation in one's life. She portrays different types of human relationships with complete authenticity. She projects the city of Lucknow as the colonial encounter between Indians and the British government. The novel is in autobiographical form and presents the Muslim culture and tradition. The writer depicts the picture of the freedom struggle and ponders over the reasons that are responsible for the riots and disturbances in society. Hosain criticises politicians for their unfair attitude towards their community and highlights the fact that how some Hindus help Muslims to save their life. Attia not only informs the reader about the good relations between the Hindus and the Muslims but also about the friendly relations of different communities including Christians. The novelist has left a ray of sunlight from the broken column of the partition.

Chapter IV *A Bend in the Ganges* introduces us to the colonial experience of Manohar Malgonkar with its serious repercussions for the colonized. The novel has an element of tragedy and reveals the main cause of the partition. *A Bend in the Ganges* is a dramatic novel that throws light on the freedom struggle as well as the partition of the sub-continent. History has obsessed Malgaonkar which is clearly shown in the novel. The novelist skilfully depicts the brutal incident of the partition with the national movement. With his keen observant power, Malgaonkar portrays pre-independent India and the hard-hearted behaviour of the British. He efficiently presents the fact that how people failed to understand the true meaning of the Gandhian principles of truth and non-violence. The inhuman behaviour of men during the partition has been portrayed vividly in the novel.

The author very powerfully presents the feeling and sentiments of the refugees

Chapter V *Azadi* showcases the pathetic picture of the bestial horrors enacted on the Indo-Pakistan border during the days of 1947. Chaman Nahal projects Sialkot in Punjab as a town where Hindus and Muslims live in amity, which is disturbed by some communal Muslims gradually. The novelist portrays those turbulent days and the ghastliness of the partition tragedy realistically. He illustrates how religion is exploited by many for serving their own purpose. However, the novel presents the optimistic attitude of the novelist. Nahal believes in moving ahead together by forgetting those days. Being a believer of humanism, Nahal has faith in the goodness of man during the time of crisis. He follows the philosophy of *Gita* which makes the novel different from other novels on the theme of the partition. The novelist has also projected the ironical role of the educated people of the country during the freedom movement. Elements of humour in the novel add to the total effect of the story. He uses symbols and images to present reality. Nahal has efficaciously conveyed the gruesomeness of the partition tragedy. The novelist impeaches both communities for the communal uneasiness and has succeeded in delineating the sudden dislocation of life and loss of harmonious atmosphere due to the partition poignantly.

Chapter VI Bapsi Sidhwa's *Ice Candy Man* is an **autobiographical novel that** reflects the perspectives of people from Pakistani on the tragic event of the partition. The novelist presents the harmonious and healthy environment of Lahore which is infected by rumours. The Muslim culture of Pakistan is deftly presented and the use of Urdu language enriches the quality of the text. The novelist crafts a sensible and balanced picture of the time of the partition in which she throws light on the politics and social atmosphere of Lahore. Sidhwa hints at the communal discord that occurred at the time of the independence among the Hindus, Muslims, and the Sikhs. Bapsi has provided some glimpses of Parsi culture also. The book also depicts characters from different religions and backgrounds that indicate the homogeneous culture of society then. The sensitive response of the partition has been revealed in the lives of people through various phases. **The awful event of the partition has been described by a handicapped child. The novel presents the feminine viewpoint and experiences with a distinctive visualization. The shifting pattern of communal relationships has been presented by a village, Pir Pindo. Sidhwa uses history to present the political conditions of Lahore at the time of the partition.**

Chapter 7 *Conclusion* refers is an analysis of the four novels research extensively. The research methodology for the study is based upon the comprehensive analysis of the novels in light of postcolonial fiction. The purpose of the study, therefore, depends mainly on four major novels which have the partition theme. All of them have handled the Partition from a postcolonial perspective and emphasise the point that the partition could not solve any problem for either of the Hindus or the Muslims. The study of the novels proves its proposition that politics plays a central role in the lives of the people and therefore finds reflection in literature. Two Pakistani novels, Mumtaz Shah Nawaz's '*The Heart Divided*' and Kamila Shamsi's '*Salt and Saffron*' have also been discussed in the conclusion. Both the novels have responded to the politics or the history of the partition at the personal as well as national level. These novels reveal the status of women in the sub-continent at the beginning of the twentieth century. Apart from these two novels, the thesis has also discussed **the women authors from Pakistan and India, Bapsi Sidhwa and Attia Hosain seem separated by more factors than just nationality. Attia writes as an Indian Muslim who does not leave India for Pakistan after the partition. Sidhwa writes as a Parsi who has stayed behind in Pakistan and subsequently moved to America. They belong, furthermore, to different generations. Sidhwa is one of those writers who while not born in August 1947 but a child at that moment, while Attia Hosain represents an older generation of partition survivors. Both women have written novels, from an upper-middle-class perspective, about women whose lives were deeply affected by the partition.**

The political and societal tension between the Hindus and Muslims led the country towards the partition. The ruinous event of the Partition brought wide-scale riots; violence that accompanied independence was a prelude to the multiple wars, coups, and governmental manipulations that plagued the area in the years that followed. The partition claimed thousands of lives and produced millions of refugees who fought for their survival against all odds. Women were directly affected during the partition. They were brutally raped and butchered. The enormous loss of human lives and property is felt even today. However, now people of both countries want peace and prosperity instead of war and destruction. Their interest lies in the healthy relations of both the countries and it is the only hope of reunion between both communities as well as countries.

www.ingramcontent.com/pod-product-compliance
Lightning Source LLC
LaVergne TN
LVHW061610070526
838199LV00078B/7233